SECONDARY SCHOOL LIBRARIAN'S ALMANAC

Activities, Bulletin Boards, and Procedures for the Whole School Year

Jane E. Streiff

THE CENTER FOR APPLIED
RESEARCH IN EDUCATION
West Nyack, New York 10995

10   9   8   7   6   5   4   3   2   1

Library of Congress Cataloging-in-Publication Data

Streiff, Jane E.
  Secondary school librarian's almanac: activities, bulletin
boards, and procedures for the whole school year / Jane E. Streiff.
    p. cm.
  1. High school libraries—Activity programs. 2. High school
libraries—Calendars. 3. School year—Calendars. 4. Bulletin
boards. I. Title.
Z675.S3S825 1989   88-35233
027.8'223--dc19   CIP

ISBN   0-87628-783-6

THE CENTER FOR APPLIED
RESEARCH IN EDUCATION
BUSINESS & PROFESSIONAL DIVISION
A division of Simon & Schuster
West Nyack, New York 10995

Printed in the United States of America

Dedicated To
Lori, Lynn, and Eric

About the Author

Jane Streiff has been a media specialist for the past twenty years in the Bethlehem Central School District, Delmar, New York. For fourteen of those years, she has been director of the media center in the high school. Before moving to New York, she was a classroom teacher in the Colorado public school system.

Her education includes a B.A. with majors in sociology and English from Cornell College, Mount Vernon, Iowa; graduate study in political science at Columbia University on a Lydia Roberts Fellowship; and an M.L.S. degree from the State University of New York at Albany.

Ms. Streiff's professional activities include conducting and participating in educational workshops and conferences as well as facilitating a Great Books discussion group. Presently, she is serving on a district committee which is studying the restructuring of school organizations. She is also a member of the Advisory Council of the Albany-Schoharie-Schenectady Board of Cooperative Educational Services School Library System.

Acknowledgments

Help from many people made this book possible. First, I wish to acknowledge the assistance and support of the media staff at Bethlehem Central High School: Kathryn Blanchard, Rosemary Brown, Ellen Dagneau, and Nicolas Nealon. I have incorporated forms and procedures which they have helped to develop over the years. Their suggestions and advice have been invaluable.

If a school media program is to be meaningful, it must have administrative support; the staff and students must use the center and its services; and teachers must be committed to integrating library research skills into the content areas. Because these conditions exist in our school, we can continue to improve and expand our media program. Our principal believes in effective library programs in schools, and has encouraged his media staff to pursue that goal.

I regret that I have been able to include only a few of the many lessons teachers in our school have developed for improving research skills. I wish to acknowledge especially the contribution to this almanac by the following persons from our district:

Margaret Dinova, Jocelyn Jerry, Andrew Joachim, John Karl, Barbara Linford, James Nehring, Shirley Schenmeyer, Joanne Smith, Susan Timmerman, Thomas Watthews, and James Yeara.

For his contribution to the appendix of forms, I am grateful to John Danek of Niskayuna High School, Niskayuna, New York.

About This Almanac

Secondary School Librarian's Almanac is designed to assist you in planning and implementing a media program which follows a natural progression through the school year, meets the needs of faculty and students, and functions as an integral part of the total school program.

Although the material in the *Almanac* is arranged in the format of a school-year calendar, it may be adapted to your particular situation. The suggestions, guides, lessons, forms, and activities included here will be helpful whether you are in a large or small secondary school library/media center, whether you are working alone or directing a staff, and whether you administer a book-oriented library or a center housing all types of media and equipment.

Secondary School Librarian's Almanac is a flexible instrument. Your own particular educational environment and the administrators to whom you report may call for revision of the timeline suggested. To make the lessons broadly applicable, room for the addition of titles from your collection has been allowed on the student worksheets. This way, the research plans can be tailored to information retrieval from sources ranging from *World Book* to machine-readable databases.

As a media specialist, you enjoy a unique and challenging role among educators. Your responsibilities require professional knowledge of content, teaching methods, and curriculum design, as well as technical competencies, managerial talent, and a high degree of positive interpersonal skills. This is quite a charge—but also quite an opportunity!

In many school environments, the library media specialist at the secondary level has a great deal of autonomy; in others, the role is quite closely prescribed. If you are in the former situation, you will want to maintain and expand your responsibilities through a highly visible, effective program. In the latter, your goal should be to establish your program through supportive services, create a need for your program, and steadily acquire the administrative trust you desire. In either case, the *Almanac* can help you reach your goal.

For each month of the school year you will find five topics: a birthday list, management tasks, library research plans, bulletin boards, and inservice and public relations. Here's a closer look at each one:

- The list of writers born during the month may suggest monthly themes or exhibits, bibliographies, or book reviews.

- Management tasks include specific responsibilities for organizing your work. This section will help you answer the question "What do I do next?" Over 50 ready-to-use, reproducible forms are included in the Appendix to help you with your work.

- Three library research plans are presented each month. These are lessons in using research tools in your media center, plus activities based on the research process. Library media skills are taught most successfully in relation to classroom studies. As you confer with classroom teachers on instructional units, these plans can be incorporated to improve the students' locational skills, their ability to select and interpret appropriate materials, and their ability to communicate. The exercises are developed at three levels of difficulty, from basic skills (Level I) to more advanced skills (Level III). You will be able to adapt the lesson plans to different subject matter or assignments if necessary.

- One or two bulletin board displays are described each month. Although a few are seasonal, they can generally be used whenever convenient and appropriate to what is going on in your school. National or widely recognized observances for each month are noted to give you other ideas for themes and displays.

- Promoting your media center and media services is an important part of your job. Activities for doing this are found in "Inservice and Public Relations."

As a library media specialist and as an educator, you understand the need for carefully developed plans for carrying out your educational programs each year. You also realize that spontaneity and flexibility are important ingredients in the successful school media program. *Secondary School Librarian's Almanac* incorporates both factors: planning and spontaneity. Use it to help you throughout the year. You'll want to keep it handy on your desk.

Jane E. Streiff

Contents

NOVEMBER • 47

DECEMBER • 65

JANUARY • 89

MAY • 167

JUNE • 185

APPENDIX • 199

September

September Birthdays

479? B.C.	Euripides
1709	Samuel Johnson
1789	James Fenimore Cooper
1828	Leo Tolstoy
1862	O. Henry
1866	H. G. Wells
1875	Edgar Rice Burroughs
1878	Upton Sinclair
1888	T. S. Eliot
1890	Agatha Christie
1896	F. Scott Fitzgerald
1897	William Faulkner
1908	Richard Wright
1911	William Golding
1924	Truman Capote
1926	John Knowles
1926	Alison Lurie
1928	Elie Wiesel
1932	Joanne Greenburg
1935	Ken Kesey
1942	Sue Ellen Bridgers
1947	Stephen King
1947	Ann Beattie

MANAGEMENT TASKS

---

*"The beginning is the most important
part of the work."*

Plato
The Republic

The management tasks for September are:

1. Preparing for opening day
2. Setting goals for your media program
3. Unpacking acquisitions

Preparing for Opening Day

You are greeted with stacks of boxes. Supplies and books, audiovisuals, new equipment, and even the first delivery of rental films will have arrived during the summer. A box was provided for the accumulation of summer correspondence; it is overflowing with the mail the main office staff placed there. Summer school teachers have returned the equipment they borrowed. Two months of periodicals fill several boxes. Does it sound familiar?

If it were not for the excitement each new school year generates, one could feel discouraged. Perhaps optimism is the by-product of the smell of new paint and floor wax. You know you must store up the feeling; it will be ten months before the school is this fresh and QUIET again!

It is important to remember, but so easy to forget, during the first few hectic days of the school year that time devoted to planning is critical, and, in the long run, well spent.

In preparing for opening day, first determine the order of tasks to be done, then who is to do them, then where and when. Ask yourself what services you will be called upon to offer as soon as your media center is open to students and teachers. A checklist of tasks ("Preparing for Opening Day") should help you get started. Space for comments has been included on the form. Throughout the year it is helpful to keep a record of your activities, observing for your own reference how well certain tasks were performed or what difficulties arose and how you resolved them. These need not be detailed narratives but simple reminders to yourself. After you have completed the procedure, drop the checklist into a manila folder in your desk. You can review these activities at the end of the year; you will be surprised and pleased with the usefulness of your comments.

"Forms to Be Duplicated" lists those forms that should be prepared and ready for opening day. Use the "Index to Forms" to locate the forms you want. They may be reproduced as they appear or adapted to your needs. It is always wise to identify the forms you duplicate with the name of your media center and the date.

Distributing hardware to teachers will be one service demanded of you immediately. Your principal, in fact, will probably request equipment for his first staff meeting. Most teachers need audiovisual equipment only occasionally; a few will use it daily. You will find some teachers will need basic equipment, such as overhead projectors, assigned to their rooms on a permanent basis.

If it is not possible for teachers to have all the equipment they use placed in their rooms for the full year, you will need to devise promptly a system for recording requests and for tracking the location of equipment so that it is shared equitably. In small schools, teachers may be willing to pick up and return the equipment they use, but if you can initiate a delivery system, using your staff or students, this is preferable. It allows for greater accessibility, fewer occasions of misplaced equipment, and it gives you the opportunity to check the condition of the pieces more regularly. Finally, delivering equipment to the teachers' rooms provides a service that is appreciated even more than doughnuts on Friday!

There are commercially prepared visual control boards for handling hardware distribution. If you lack such a board, you may devise one by attaching book pockets to a bulletin board for holding the equipment control cards while the equipment is out in use. A room map of the school can be enlarged, and colored pins can be used to show at a glance the location of various pieces. Use a color-code scheme to designate types of equipment. If your inventory is small and equipment must be moved to be shared during a day, this is an excellent system for assessing quickly the location of the piece of equipment in demand. A third way to manage the distribution of equipment is to keep the control cards in a card file with dividers which separate the cards by type of equipment.

Start out the year by asking your faculty to request equipment at least twenty-four hours in advance of need. You must have that kind of leadtime to anticipate and arrange delivery and pickup. Some requests will always arise more spontaneously; that is the nature of teaching. You handle these requests in a cheerful, cooperative manner but never deviate from the obligation to service first requests first.

Transfer the teachers' requests from the request forms to a loose-leaf notebook. The page of deliveries and pickups for a particular day can then be removed and used by staff or students charged with these tasks. The best time for handling delivery is before or after school. It is satisfying to a teacher to find the projector he requested there in his room upon arrival in the morning. Nothing is more frustrating to a teacher than to be faced with tracking down his request or altering lesson plans between the time the first bell rings and his class arrives.

Keep the copies of teachers' requests for equipment in a file for reference in the event there is confusion about who asked for what; and, later in the year, these requests provide valuable statistics for your annual report or for budget development.

Now, if you have used the task list provided, you have . . . ascertained that your facility is clean and in order, you have acquired the forms you need to get started, you have made sure that your staff has the necessary supplies, you have put up two bulletin boards, you have scheduled your staff's time so that stations are covered, you have posted near the desk the information you will refer to many times in the first month of school, and you have filled teacher requests for equipment.

You are ready!

Setting Goals

You, as the administrator of a school library media center, have four major goals for which to strive:

- Selecting and acquiring, organizing and making accessible instructional materials to support the educational program of the school
- Planning for and implementing use of those materials
- Promoting use of the media center by students and faculty for many and diverse educational purposes
- Providing instruction to students in skills which will enable them to retrieve information, select appropriate sources, and communicate ideas

With these broad goals in mind, you should proceed to develop more specific objectives for the school year. Your objectives—and the policies and procedures for attaining them—must conform to the policies and philosophies of the total school.

Obtain the following documents for study:

- Board of Education Policy Manual
- Faculty handbook
- Student handbook
- State Education Department guidelines
- Media Center records and reports from previous years

Ask yourself: In what way do I want media services to be different in June from the way they are in September?

Be realistic. You may not have staff nor time to present a skills lesson to every English class in the school, but it may be possible to do so for all ninth grades, or for all Expository Writing classes, for example.

It may be unrealistic to hope for a new budget that is double the one you are working with in September, but an increase of ten percent would be a reasonable expectation and one which could be readily justified.

State your goals in writing, giving the action required; then set a time for initiating your plan.

Example:

Objective	To place a media specialist on the school's curriculum committee this year.
Action	Compose a memo to the principal suggesting that such an invitation be extended. State the contributions a school media specialist can make to the process of curriculum development.
When	Third week in September. Most curriculum committees start their work early in the fall; check the principal's calendar.

Turn your day-by-day desk calendar (National School Calendar is a good one) into a "tickler file." Using removable self-stick note pads, place one sheet at the edge of the day you have set as your deadline for a task. Let the sheet protrude from the calendar page, with your reminder printed there. Since these notes may be purchased in a variety of colors, you may devise a code which will alert you at a glance to the message: Memos or reports due, meetings, lessons scheduled for presentation.

When you have determined the major aspects of your program, you are ready to assign responsibilities and duties to your staff in order to carry out that program. The underlying principles for development of these assignments should be: Maximize the amount of time for media specialists and paraprofessionals to serve students and teachers directly. The clerical, or non-instructional, staff time available to you should be devoted to those duties which support your services. Decide which responsibilities should be shared and which are handled more efficiently by one person. The following division of labor may work for you:

Professional Responsibilities

- Provide reference service to students
- Coordinate work assignments
- Provide liaison with administration and staff
- Develop and control media center budget
- Provide library skills instruction
- Provide inservice for teachers
- Select materials for purchase
- Supervise processing of materials
- Supervise shelving and maintenance of materials
- Develop a vertical file
- Provide exhibits and displays
- Supervise reserve procedures
- Maintain audiovisual equipment inventory
- Classify materials for access
- Supervise circulation procedures
- Recommend hardware and software for purchase
- Produce media
- Develop instructional television programming
- Supervise delivery of equipment and non-print materials
- Evaluate program
- Interpret media program to staff and community
- Develop automation procedures
- Supervise maintenance of the media center

Clerical Duties

- Open and close the media center
- Check in materials
- Supply work stations
- Retrieve magazines

- Keep budget records
- Repair materials and equipment
- Type cards, memos, correspondence, and orders
- File documents
- Process materials for circulation
- Deliver equipment
- Record and play back video programs
- Process requests for equipment, video playback, films
- Clip, prepare and file vertical file materials
- Record circulation statistics
- Prepare overdue notices
- Provide duplication service
- Enter data in computer
- Supervise students as necessary

Unpacking Acquisitions

During September, you will need to turn your attention to unpacking and checking in new materials. Both students and teachers will be eager to see new books and magazines. The audiovisual materials very likely will have been purchased to support new courses in the curriculum and will be needed immediately. Some administrators recognize this need for materials and provide summer clerical help in the media center. However, since media specialists invariably work the same contract year as teachers, the verification of the summer work and the professional classification and preparation of the materials for the shelf remain to be done after school opens. This lack of summer work is the single most compelling reason for ordering, pre-processed, all materials possible.

Develop standard procedures for unpacking orders and put these procedures into writing so that no steps are missed and uniformity can be assured no matter who is doing the work.

No processing of an order should be started until the order is verified and an invoice has arrived. Invoices usually come separately from an order and many times will go directly to the business office. Packing slip prices may vary from the invoice so they should not be used for verification of an order.

The following procedures for unpacking orders are general enough to get you started:

A.   *Unpacking a Book Order*
1. Check the invoice number against the label on the box.
2. Pull the original order from the file.
3. As you unpack each book:
    a. Check it off on the packing slip.
    b. Check it off on the invoice.
    c. Record the price from the invoice in pencil on the book card under title, on the shelf list card, and in the upper right-hand corner of the book's title page.
    d. If the book was not pre-processed, note the price on the title page only.

4. Pull the order cards for the books from the ''want'' file. Place each card in the appropriate book.

5. Collect the books for the media specialist to proceed with cataloging procedures.

6. Mark the purchase order with the date and initial it.

7. Send the purchase order with the invoice to the business office for payment to the vendor.

B. *Unpacking Audiovisual Software*

1. Check the invoice number against the label on the box.

2. Check your purchase order against the invoice.

3. Unpack the audiovisual material:

   a. Verify that all components are included.
   b. Test each component.

4. If the program is unacceptable, pack it for return.

5. If material was pre-processed, note price on the shelf card and on the circulation card.

6. If not pre-processed, note price on the order card and place card with box.

7. Route to the media specialist for cataloging.

8. Initial and date copy of the purchase order, and send to the business office for payment to the vendor.

C. *Checking in New Magazine Subscriptions*

1. Check the price against the invoice.

2. Mark the purchase order with the date and initial it. Send it to the business office for payment.

3. Prepare an inventory card for the periodical log.

4. Type the following information on the card:

   a. Date first issue is received
   b. Term of the subscription
   c. Frequency of issues
   d. Price of subscription
   e. Price of individual copies

5. Stamp the magazine with your property stamp.

6. Stamp date received on the magazine.

7. Mark date of issue in upper left-hand corner of the magazine. (White pressure-sensitive labels may be needed for clarity.)

8. The media specialist will indicate on the inventory card:

   a. Whether the magazine is to be routed
   b. Where it is to be filed
   c. Articles to be shared with staff

9. File the inventory card alphabetically by title in the periodical log.

D.   *Checking-in New Equipment*
1. Check the invoice number against the label of the shipping carton.
2. Check the purchase order against the packing slip.
3. Indicate on the purchase order the date of unpacking.
4. Verify that the equipment conforms to specifications.
5. Test the equipment.
6. Initial the purchase order and send to the business office for payment to vendor.
7. Identify the equipment as school property by marking with a permanent marker, etching, or applying school property labels.
8. Prepare an inventory card for the equipment.
9. Assign a control number.
10. Attach a pocket to the equipment with permanent sealing tape.
11. Type a control card, giving a number, type of equipment, and serial number.
12. Share the information on the inventory card with the person in charge of insurance reports.
13. Stamp the operator's manual with a property stamp.
14. File all equipment manuals for quick access.

LIBRARY RESEARCH PLANS

Level I: Card Catalog Review

The following are the objectives for this library research plan:

- The students will review the process of locating materials through the card catalog.
- The students will be able to differentiate among these types of cards: Author, Title, Subject, "See" and "See also," Reference, Nonprint or Audiovisual.
- The students will review the Dewey Decimal system of classification.
- The students will demonstrate the ability to use the card catalog by completing a brief exercise.

Media Center
Level I
Card Catalog Review

The materials included in this lesson may be produced as overhead projection transparencies. Or you may duplicate multiple copies of the pages for distribution to the class.

Arrange the materials in order from Figure 1-1 through Figure 1-8, and prepare your remarks accordingly. The lesson is brief and should take no more than ten minutes to present. The materials should be familiar to secondary school students, but using these few specific illustrations will offer you the opportunity to bring into your presentation any circulation procedures, special shelving arrangements, and additional designations on the call numbers which you wish to stress. Encourage the students to question you as you proceed, and ask them to share the differences they observe from their previous library experiences.

Stress the card catalog as the source for information about the location of all materials in the media center.

Level II: *Facts on File*®

The objectives for this library research plan are as follow:

- The students will learn the location of *Facts on File*.
- The students will learn to use *Facts on File* independently to retrieve information.
- The students will be able to use the *Facts on File* index as a quick reference for facts.
- The students will demonstrate their ability to use *Facts on File* by completing a brief exercise.

Your introduction to the lesson should include this information:

1. *Facts on File* is a weekly news digest of worldwide reporting from 50 newspapers and magazines. It is indexed twice monthly. Printed on white paper, *Facts on File* is a key to subjects, people, organizations, and countries, and is a source for a full-color world atlas.
2. The indexes are printed on blue paper, and are cumulated quarterly and annually on yellow paper. Arranged by subject, the indexes are cross-referenced and are useful as quick references for dates and specific information.
3. A table of contents is printed on the front page of each weekly issue.
4. Explanations on how to use this source appear with each index.
5. A key to abbreviations appears with each index.
6. Each entry in the index includes a description of the event reported in the news digest, and gives the month and day of the event. Each entry also includes the marginal letter by the report in the digest and the column in the digest where the report is printed.

Figure 1-9 is a sample and Figure 1-10 is a *Facts on File* exercise for your students.

Level III: NewsBank®

The following are the objectives for this library research plan:

- The students will learn the location of NewsBank® and the microfiche reader.
- The students will learn to retrieve information from the NewsBank® microfiche file by using the indexes.
- The students will learn to use the microfiche reader.
- The students will read and interpret information from more than one source.
- The students will learn how the NewsBank® index can be used to narrow a research topic.
- The students will learn the correct form for citing NewsBank® in a bibliography.

• The students will demonstrate competency in using this source by completing an exercise.

Your introduction to the lesson should include this information:

1. NewsBank® is a source of information about current affairs with data selected from newspapers in over 450 U.S. cities. In microfiche format, NewsBank® is updated monthly, indexed, and filed by color code.

2. NewsBank® covers major current issues, worldwide opinion, broad interest areas, and biographies.

3. NewsBank® indexes are printed monthly and cumulated quarterly and annually. Organized alphabetically by subject, NewsBank® is useful in focusing your topic.

4. NewsBank® articles are grouped by subject and are color-coded for easy access in broad areas.

Figure 1-11 is an informational sheet you can give to your students. Then make copies of Figures 1-12 and 1-13 and have your students complete the exercise.

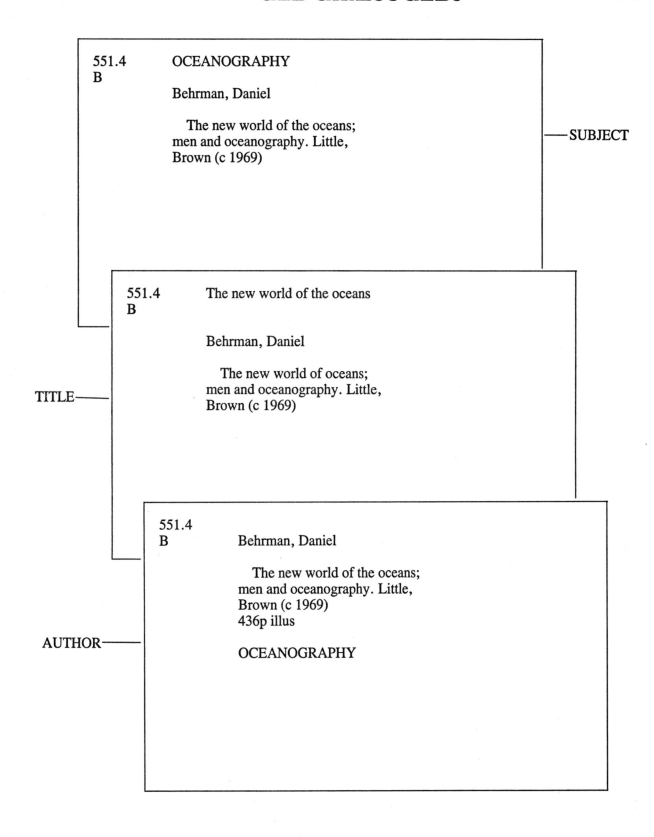

551.4
B

OCEANOGRAPHY

Behrman, Daniel

    The new world of the oceans;
men and oceanography. Little,
Brown (c 1969)

— SUBJECT

551.4
B

The new world of the oceans

Behrman, Daniel

    The new world of oceans;
men and oceanography. Little,
Brown (c 1969)

TITLE—

551.4
B

Behrman, Daniel

    The new world of the oceans;
men and oceanography. Little,
Brown (c 1969)
436p illus

OCEANOGRAPHY

AUTHOR—

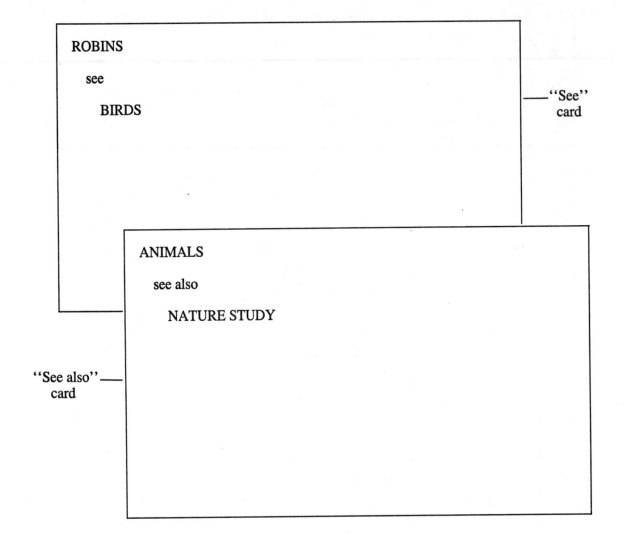

ROBINS

   see

      BIRDS

— "See" card

ANIMALS

   see also

      NATURE STUDY

"See also" — card

599.5
ELL

Ellis, Richard

The book of whales, written and illus by Richard
Ellis. Knopf (c 1980)
202p illus (part col)

Ellis, accomplished both as an artist and as a
scientific writer, reproduces a number of his
paintings of the world's largest mammals and
describes the behavior, habitats, and
characteristics of thirty-three species.
Bibliog

Whales I T

EUROPE - HISTORY

R
309.1

Mitchell, B. R.

European historical statistics 1750-1975; second
revised edition.
Facts on File, 1980.
868p.

STATISTICS - YEARBOOKS
EUROPE - HISTORY
EUROPE - STATISTICS

Kit
973.8
NAT

U.S. - EMIGRATION AND IMMIGRATION

Nation of immigrants (Filmstrip) Guidance
Associates of Pleasantville, NY, 1967.

Summary: Traces the history of immigration in the
United States and describes important features of
the immigration laws.

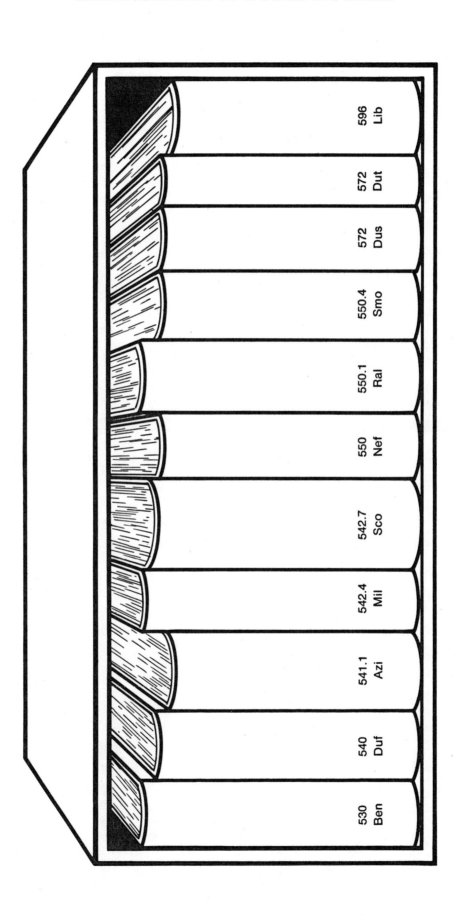

Use the card catalog to answer the following. Record your answers on the "Card Catalog Answer Sheet."

1. Write the call number, author, and title for one book about _____

    _____ .
    (subject entry)

2. Write the publisher and title using the main entry card for a book by _____

    _____ .
    (author entry)

3. Write the call number and copyright date for the book entitled _____

    _____ .
    (title entry)

4. What subject heading would you use for a book about _____

    _____ ?
    (cross reference)

5. Write the call number and title of an audiovisual program about _____

    _____ .
    (audiovisual format)

6. After checking the subject heading _____, you should *also* check

    this subject _____ for information.
    (cross reference)

Name _____   Class _____

Date _____

CARD CATALOG ANSWER SHEET   1–8

Use this answer sheet to record your answers to the "Card Catalog Exercise."

1. Call number _____

   Author _____

   Title _____

2. Publisher _____

   Title _____

3. Call number _____

   Copyright date _____

4. Subject heading _____

5. Call number _____

   Title _____

6. Cross reference _____

GLOSSARY DIAGRAM FOR BOLDFACED WORDS IN TEXT

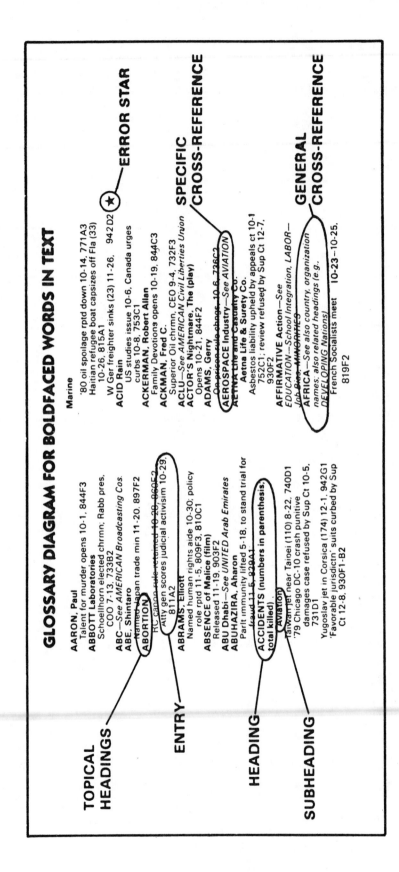

TOPICAL HEADINGS

ENTRY

HEADING

SUBHEADING

ERROR STAR

SPECIFIC CROSS-REFERENCE

GENERAL CROSS-REFERENCE

AARON, Paul
Talent for murder opens 10-1. 844F3
ABBOTT Laboratories
Schoellhorn elected chrmn; Rabb pres.
 COO 7-13. 733B2
ABE, Shintaro
 Named Japan trade min 11-20. 897F2
ABORTION
 RC Canon rule restored 10-28, 960E2
 Atty gen scores judicial activism 10-29,
 811A2
ABRAMS, Elliott
 Named human rights aide 10-30; policy
 role rptd 11-5, 809F3, 810C1
ABSENCE of Malice (film)
 Released 11-19. 903F2
ABU Dhabi—*See UNITED Arab Emirates*
ABUHAZIRA, Aharon
 Parlt immunity lifted 5-18, to stand trial for
 fraud 11-5, 829A1
**ACCIDENTS (numbers in parenthesis,
 total killed)**
 Aviation
 Taiwan jet near Taipei (110) 8-22, 740D1
 '79 Chicago DC-10 crash punitive
 damages case refused by Sup Ct 10-5,
 731D1
 Yugoslav jet in Corsica (174) 12-1, 942G1
 'Favorable jurisdictn' suits curbed by Sup
 Ct 12-8, 930F1-B2

 Marine
 '80 oil spoilage rptd down 10-14, 771A3
 Haitian refugee boat capsizes off Fla (33)
 10-26, 815A1
 W Ger freighter sinks (23) 11-26,   942D2 (★)
ACID Rain
 US studies issue 10-6, Canada urges
 curbs 10-8, 753C1
ACKERMAN, Robert Allen
 Family Devotions opens 10-19, 844C3
ACKMAN, Fred C.
 Superior Oil chrmn, CEO 9-4, 732F3
ACLU—*See AMERICAN Civil Liberties Union*
ACTOR'S Nightmare, The (play)
 Opens 10-21, 844F2
ADAMS, Gerry
 Convicted, rule shone 10-6, 726C2
AEROSPACE Industry—*See AVIATION*
AETNA Life and Casualty Co.
 Aetna Life & Surety Co.
 Asbestos liability upheld by appeals ct 10-1
 752C1; review refused by Sup Ct 12-7.
 930F2
AFFIRMATIVE Action—See
 EDUCATION—School Integration, LABOR—
 Job Bias MINORITIES
AFRICA—See also country, organization
 names; also related headings (e.g.
 DEVELOPING Nations)
 French Socialists meet   10-23–10-25.
 819F2

Name _____ Class _____

Date _____

FACTS ON FILE EXERCISE   1–10

1. Select the *Facts on File* binder for 19 _____.

2. Locate this subject in the index: _____ .

3. Enter the location of the news in the news digest:

    a. Page Number _____

    b. Date _____

    c. Marginal Letter _____

    d. Column _____

4. Locate the news item and identify the weekly issue:

    a. Volume _____

    b. Number _____

   You have now retrieved information about a specific topic in the current events resource called *Facts on File*. By collecting the data about the location of the information, you have provided yourself with the information you would need to include this source in a bibliography.

   When completed, return this sheet to your library media specialist and discuss any problems you may have had in using *Facts on File*.

CURRENT ISSUES AND EVENTS FROM NEWSPAPERS IN OVER 450 U.S. CITIES

HOW TO USE NewsBank®

1 ▶ **LOCATE YOUR RESEARCH TOPIC.** The NewsBank Index is arranged alphabetically by name or subject. The form below illustrates how to jot down the information underlined in the sample index entry to locate articles on the microfiche.

Main subject heading   Subheading

DRUG LAWS AND ENFORCEMENT
   laboratories, illegal
   PCP
     California - 1987 LAW 7:D6-8

Secondary subheading

YEAR OF INDEX

MICROFICHE GRID COORDINATES
(i.e., row and column number on microfiche)

MICROFICHE CATEGORY

Geographic origin of event or issue

MICROFICHE CARD NUMBER

TOPIC	YEAR OF INDEX	MICROFICHE CATEGORY	MICROFICHE CARD NUMBER	MICROFICHE GRID COORDINATES
Drug Laws	1987	LAW	7	D6-8

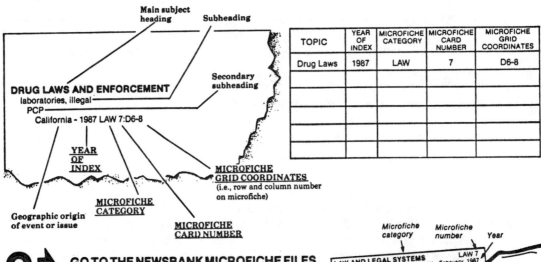

Microfiche category   Microfiche number   Year

LAW AND LEGAL SYSTEMS   LAW 7
NewsBank, Inc. copyright 1987   Vol. XVIII   February 1987

LAW 7:D6

2 ▶ **GO TO THE NEWSBANK MICROFICHE FILES.** Select your microfiche using the year, the microfiche category and the microfiche number.

3 ▶ **PLACE THE MICROFICHE IN A READER.** The letter and number of the grid coordinates (article location) appear in the lower left corner of each frame.

CITING NEWSBANK

Since NewsBank gathers and reformats information first published elsewhere, the bibliographic citation needs to be in a special form. Following is an example of a citation derived from Eugene B. Fleischer, **A Style Manual for Citing Microform and Nonprint Media** (Chicago: American Library Association, 1978).

Footnote:
⁵Kristina Horton, "Do-It-Yourself Illegal Drug Labs on Rise, Proving Deadly," Torrance (California) Daily Breeze, February 1, 1987 (Located in NewsBank [Microform], Law and Legal Systems, 1987, 7:D6-8, fiche).

Bibliography:
Horton, Kristina, "Do-It-Yourself Illegal Drug Labs on Rise, Proving Deadly," Torrance (California) Daily Breeze, February 1, 1987 (Located in NewsBank [Microform], Law and Legal Systems, 1987, 7:D6-8, fiche).

NewsBank,® inc. 58 Pine Street, New Canaan, CT 06840

NEWSBANK® EXERCISE   1–12

1. Locate the NewsBank® index for 19 _____.

2. Locate a subject heading of your choice and write it here:

   _____

3. Indicate the location of two articles you would like to read about that subject:

   Article 1

   a. Geographic origin of event _____

   b. Microfiche category _____

   c. Microfiche card number _____

   d. Microfiche grid coordinates:

      Row _____

      Column number _____

   Article 2

   a. Geographic origin of event _____

   b. Microfiche category _____

   c. Microfiche card number _____

   d. Microfiche grid coordinates:

      Row _____

      Column number _____

4. Place the microfiche on the reader and read the selected articles. NOTE: If you are unsure about how to use the microfiche reader, see the sheet ''How to Use the Microfiche Reader.''

1–12 cont'd.

5. Write the bibliographic citations for the two articles you have read:

   Article 1

   a. Footnote—_____

   _____

   _____

   _____

   b. Bibliography—_____

   _____

   _____

   _____

   Article 2

   a. Footnote—_____

   _____

   _____

   _____

   b. Bibliography—_____

   _____

   _____

   _____

6. Go back to the index and locate the following subject heading:

   _____

7. Choose and list here a subheading that would allow you to focus on a more specific aspect of the subject:

   _____

   When completed, return this sheet to your library media specialist and discuss any problems you may have had in using NewsBank® .

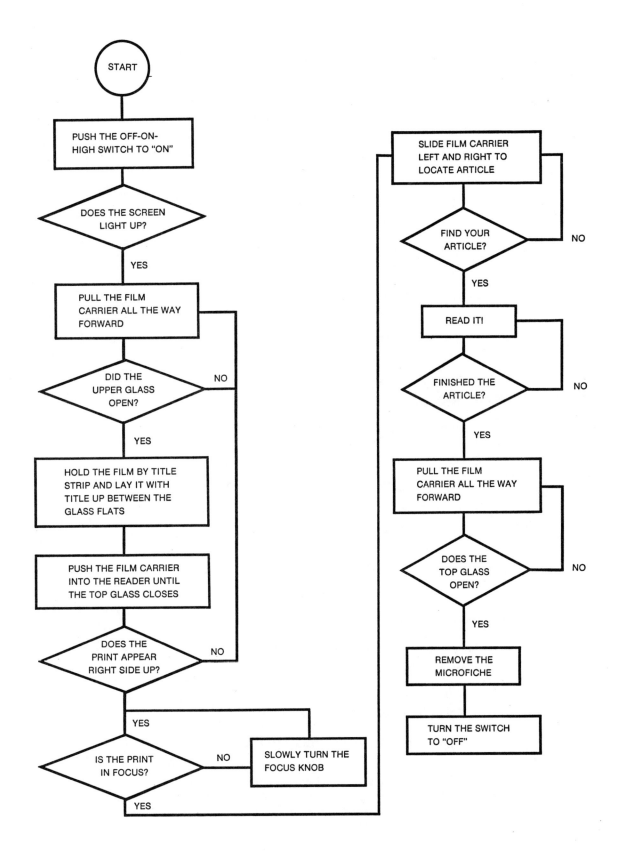

SEPTEMBER BULLETIN BOARDS

Labor Day
Grandparents' Day
Hispanic Heritage Week
World Peace Day
National Anthem Day
Harvest Moon Days
Good Neighbor Day
American Indian Day
International Literacy Day

Of Current Interest

In September, establish a bulletin board which you reserve for announcements and information of current interest. Items to be included there are:

- Media center rules of conduct
- Circulation policies
- Daily bulletin
- Floor plan of the school
- Fire drill instructions
- Media center floor plan
- School calendar
- School menu
- Official club news

A word of caution: You should require that permission be granted for posting announcements or information on this bulletin board. Most secondary schools have bulletin boards in cafeterias, lounging areas, or halls where students can "sound off."

Live Dangerously—READ

To prepare a "Live Dangerously—READ" bulletin board you will need:

- Black construction paper
- White construction paper
- Posters or pictures of action sports

1. Cut large white letters spelling your bulletin board caption.
2. Cover the bulletin board with black construction paper. On that background, place your caption and a collage of pictures of people enjoying sports as participants. You might want to check with the yearbook advisor for pictures of students in school sports.

3. Draw round ''speech'' balloons out of white construction paper. On each balloon, write ''I've read _____'' (adding a title from your collection on each balloon).

4. Attach the balloons near the pictures. Change the captions during the time you have this bulletin board on display.

The American Library Association has established an annual ''Banned Books Week.'' It occurs in September and is co-sponsored by the Association of American Publishers, National Association of College Stores, the American Booksellers Association, and the American Society of Journalists and Authors.

The theme for the week is intellectual freedom, freedom guaranteed by the First Amendment to our Constitution. You can acquire a ''Banned Books Week'' kit from ALA. The kits have many suggestions for celebrating the freedom to read and for bringing attention to the dangers of restraining a people's right to a free press and free access to information and opinion. The kits contain attractive posters and ideas for innovative displays and activities. Your state library media association also will have materials on this subject.

Selecting titles of banned books, as publicized by ALA in these kits or in issues of the *Newsletter on Intellectual Freedom*, would make an emphatic statement in your ''Live Dangerously—READ'' bulletin board. I recommend that you take time to become familiar with your school and community first. I suggest, also, that you discuss such a plan with the English supervisor in your school as well as your principal.

If you choose to emphasize banned books in your display you may add to your bulletin board these items:

- A facsimile of the First Amendment (available in the ''Banned Books Week'' kit)
- A typed or hand-lettered ''dangerous books'' list

INSERVICE AND PUBLIC RELATIONS: ORIENTATION TO THE MEDIA CENTER

Orientation to the media center for new teachers and new students is a priority in your September program of activities. Your principal may anticipate this need and schedule your orientation during the first days of school. If not, contact new teachers on your own with an invitation for a brief inservice session. You will need to arrange for new students to come to the media center from class. These arrangements should be made with the department chairpersons. Bringing students in from English class is appropriate, and generally those teachers appreciate this introduction to the media center for their students in advance of research assignments and skills instruction.

After you have firmed up your schedule for new teacher and student orientations, plan carefully for your presentations. A few general suggestions for both audiences are:

1. Send a reminder to the teachers involved at least two days before the sessions.

2. Send a copy of the schedule for orientation to your principal, inviting him or her to attend.

3. Extend an invitation to returning teachers, also.

4. Share your plans with your staff, requesting that they be available during orientation.

5. Invite a student from the school newspaper staff.

With both teachers and students, you should:

- Be brief.
- Be friendly.
- Be confident (prepared)!

Certain information should be included in your presentations to both audiences:

- Media center hours
- Circulation procedures
- Policies regarding overdues and lost materials
- Introduction of the media center staff
- Access for students (passes, unscheduled time)
- Special media center activities (such as planning a club)
- Behavior expected of students in the media center
- Interlibrary loan procedures
- General location of materials

The new teachers will also want to know:

- How to arrange for equipment delivery
- How to order films
- How to arrange for class use of the media center
- What special services you offer teachers, such as ERIC searches, selection tools, bibliographies, preview of materials, reserve collections, periodical routing, bulletin board materials, skills instruction, and use of exhibit facilities

Handouts that would be appreciated at your orientation sessions include:

- A list of periodical holdings
- An outline or brochure describing services
- A bibliography of new fiction
- A bibliography of your professional collection
- Bookmarks
- A floor plan of the media center
- An outline of topics you cover in skills lessons

Although you can present your information in a talk, you may want to enhance your presentation with slides. This is easier than you might think. Take a few pictures that can serve as a travelogue of the media center and will illustrate some of the points in your talk. Include a picture of the staff and try to get shots that show students using the media center. Many processing studios will develop film in hours, so adding slides to your talk is possible even though preparation time is short in September. If you do not feel confident taking pictures, give this job to someone else for next year. Get acquainted with the students in photography class, or perhaps someone on your staff can take good photos.

Once you have slides of your media center, you can elaborate on your program for another time by recording your narration on an audiocassette. You will find that repeating your presentations to several classes is not an easy task, and a recording will be a relief. A slide/tape presentation does, however, remove some of the spontaneity from your orientation.

Remember one of the first suggestions made about these orientation sessions—be brief! Both teachers and students will appreciate time to look around after your talk.

There always will be students who will enter school during the year. Ask the registrar to send you the name and homeroom number of each new student. Contact the student by means of a note to homeroom, inviting him or her to the media center during unscheduled time. Welcome new students to the school with a personalized tour of the media center.

Orientation to your media center and the services you are prepared to offer, along with the introduction of the personnel on your staff, is positive, effective public relations.

If your principal and a school newspaper reporter respond to your invitations and are able to attend one of the orientations, both will learn something about media services they did not know before. That will be newsworthy to the student, and your principal will appreciate the information about such an important part of the school program.

October

"Ye cannot rival for one hour
October's bright blue weather."

Helen Hunt Jackson
October's Bright Blue Weather

October Birthdays

1340	Geoffrey Chaucer
1751	Richard Sheridan
1758	Noah Webster
1772	Samuel Taylor Coleridge
1830	Helen Hunt Jackson
1854	Oscar Wilde
1888	Eugene O'Neill
1890	Conrad Richter
1900	Thomas Wolfe
1902	Arna Bontemps
1904	Graham Greene
1910	Ester Wier
1915	Arthur Miller
1919	Doris Lessing
1923	Desmond Bagley
1929	Ursula Le Guin
1931	John LeCarre
1932	Katherine Paterson
1932	Sylvia Plath
1934	Le Roi Jones
1941	Anne Tyler
1942	Michael Crichton

MANAGEMENT TASKS

*"The reward of a thing well done,
is to have done it."*

Ralph Waldo Emerson
New England Reformers

The management tasks for October are:

1. Cataloging new materials
2. Revising your catalog
3. Housing materials

Cataloging New Materials

In September, you prepared for opening days, and now you have your media program successfully underway. You set a few broad, achievable goals, and you are already thinking about their implementation.

You unpacked your acquisitions and now you must prepare new materials for circulation. When cataloging new materials, there are several options available to you:

1. You may obtain pre-processing of materials when you purchase them. This is an effective option, especially if your clerical or aide time is limited. The materials may be purchased "shelf ready," or with cataloging kits which require a minimum of work affixing the provided pockets and labels. You must verify the cataloging the vendor has provided.

2. You may purchase catalog cards from another source, such as the Library of Congress. This will entail a waiting period between the time you have procured the materials and your order for cards arrives. Again, you must verify the cataloging against your catalog. If you obtain your cards from the Library of Congress the subject headings will necessarily differ from other cataloging authorities, such as *Sears*.

3. You may subscribe to machine-readable cataloging from a database. If you have a computer in your media center, or readily available in your building for your use, this is a swift, accurate source. Costly.

4. Finally, you may catalog the materials yourself. This is a satisfying, professional task, and one that you may choose to pursue, given time and clerical assistance. Most books now printed in the United States offer cataloging-in-publication (CIP). This information is printed on the back of a book's title page. Other aids to original cataloging are: the Dewey classifications to be found in *Sears* (Thirteenth and succeeding editions), H. W. Wilson Company's standard catalogs for schools, and union catalogs.

The chances are you may use all of the options mentioned to catalog new materials. Even though you purchase materials pre-processed there are always some for which the vendor does not provide cataloging.

Whatever procedures you adopt for cataloging new materials, I offer the following general observations about this task:

• Develop your card catalog as your authority. Do not be afraid to disagree with the cataloging offered by other sources.

• It is important to take time as you catalog materials to examine them thoroughly. Unacceptable bindings, transposed or missing pages, and defective components in audiovisual programs are all problems you may encounter, and the materials should be returned and exchanged even though to do so is a nuisance.

• Examine the material for content. Familiarize yourself with the scope and authority of the material by checking the index and the table of contents. At this time, note on the order card, which you are keeping with the materials, the names of department heads or other staff members who will be interested in this acquisition.

• When classifying materials prepare the information for your typist on three-inch by five-inch slips. This size slip will fit into any of your filing arrangements. Write or print carefully, since some of the typist's work will be done without the materials at hand. It is possible your typist will be able to complete the preparation of catalog cards using technologies other than the typewriter. A master card may be typed on ''multi-strip'' cards available for duplication on a copying machine. Computer programs, also, are available for printing catalog cards. In either case you will plan for your typist to type or keyboard information in batches, and your three inch by five inch slip will be, for a time, the source for the cataloging information even after the material is in circulation.

• Note on the order cards the classification numbers you have given each item. A file of these order cards, kept at the circulation desk, will help you locate new materials until all cards are prepared and filed in your catalog. New materials will be in demand; locating them quickly is essential.

• Add the Library of Congress (LC) number and the International Standard Book Numbers (ISBN) to your cataloging whenever they are available in the material. You will find many uses for these numbers in the future. They will allow you to access the information needed to load your collection into a machine-readable database; they are being used in networking and collective collection development by regions; they facilitate replacing materials.

• If you are producing cards with a computer program, store the files on disks and save the disks. Some automated circulation systems will allow you to load this data at a future time into the system, thus saving time when you are ready to put your card catalog into a machine-readable database.

A. *Procedures for Pre-Processed Materials*
   1. Check the card catalog to see whether the material is a duplicate.

   2. If a duplicate, verify that the call numbers conform and that all cards are in the catalog:

      a. Pull the old shelf card.
      b. Add new accession number and price.

   3. If the material is a duplicate and a discrepancy exists in the cataloging:

      a. Pull all cards.
      b. Place cards with material.
      c. Set aside for original cataloging.

4. If title is not a duplicate, proceed to verify classification:
   a. Determine the accuracy in cataloging authority.
   b. Determine appropriateness for your collection.
   c. Check for errors in the processing kit.

5. Note for the typist any changes or additions to the assigned number.
6. Check subject headings against your authority and catalog.
7. Check on the shelf list card the subject headings and added entries you wish used.
8. If any subject headings are new to your catalog, place a penciled check by them in *Sears* (or the authority you are using) for reference as you catalog other materials.
9. Add your property stamp to the material. Mark all components of audiovisual materials with a permanent marker or stamp.
10. Add call numbers and special designations to the spine of the book or to dust jacket, and to housing of audiovisual materials.
11. Add any special designations to all cards.
12. Add LC numbers and ISBNs to the shelf card.
13. Note the call number on the order card.
14. Secure the material for your security system.
15. Add the title of the new acquisition to any appropriate bibliographies.
16. Add the accession number of material to:
    a. Shelf card
    b. Title page
    c. Book pocket
    d. Book card
17. Attach the book pocket to the flyleaf or inside cover. Attach the book pocket to the inside of the audiovisual program housing.
18. Add a clear book jacket to the book's dust jacket.
19. Optional: Add color-coded strips to top edge of cards for audiovisual materials.
20. Separate the cards for filing.
21. Alphabetize author/title and subject cards.
22. Arrange shelf cards by classification.
23. File the cards.
24. Alphabetize order cards by title.
25. File order cards at the circulation desk.

B. *Procedures for Original Cataloging*
   1. Check the card catalog for duplication of title.
   2. If a duplicate, proceed as for pre-processed material.
   3. If the title is in a series:

a. Pull all cards.

b. Add new edition to cards.

c. Add new accession number and price to shelf card.

4. If a new title, proceed to catalog.

5. Consult CIP and other sources.

6. Compare suggested classifications to your catalog.

7. Check the classification in your authority schedules.

8. Check subject headings for accuracy and conformity.

9. Write the cataloging information on a slip. Use title entry for audiovisuals.

10. Note special designations for the typist.

11. Suggested audiovisual designations:

FS   – Filmstrip

CP   – Computer Program

SFS – Sound filmstrip

F   – Film

FL   – Filmloop

SG   – Simulation game

MF – Microform

M   – Model

SL   – Slides

SSL – Sound slides

AC   – Audiocassette

VC   – Videocassette

R-R – Reel-to-reel audiotape

TR   – Transparency

SP   – Study print

REC – Phonodisc

Revising Your Catalog

As you do original cataloging of new materials, or as you verify the cataloging from other sources, it will become apparent that classification schemes are not static. The tools you are using will be different with each edition as the editors attempt to meet the demands of this burgeoning information age. Access to new topics and new fields of knowledge require expanded and altered classifications, and new entries to sources. You know, from filing in your catalog, that even the simplest addition or deletion of a word or letter in a subject heading can place the entry in a different spot in your catalog from similar entries.

This problem of whether to revise your catalog to conform to new classifications is one which will not disappear. Revision has to take place in some fashion. Your pre-processed materials will be revised; the sources you use as aids to cataloging will be revised. You have a choice of accepting new forms and revising old ones, or changing the new ones to conform the old. You will want to keep up with change; if you were to choose the latter course, revision problems would increase with every new acquisition.

The task is not as grim as it first appears. Accept the fact that you cannot work miracles and that you need not undertake sweeping revisions.

First, decide whether the change in your catalog is a critical one. Adding an expanded number to a few books may not be too grand a task. The time you can devote to reclassifying, and the amount of clerical help you have should be factors in your decision, also. If your collection is small you may revise with relative ease. Consider the fact, however, that most changes in cataloging schemes can be handled with cross-references. If you provide clear directions from one spot to another in your catalog you can accommodate many revisions without changing the materials or the cards.

Once you decide to revise the cataloging of materials in your collection these procedures should be helpful:

1. Gather the materials on a book cart

2. Pull all cards for each item

3. Work with a single item at a time and follow the task to completion

4. Keep the pulled cards with the materials until the revision is completed

5. Prepare instructions for the typist on a slip

6. Change call numbers on all cards, book pockets, and charge cards

7. If subject headings are revised, the new headings must be indicated in place of the old on all cards

8. Correct the call numbers on any bibliographies which include the material

You may find it is easier to produce a new set of cards than to work with the old. This is especially true if you are printing your cards on a computer. If there is a record of the obsolete cataloging data in a computer data file, you can reenter the file, make the necessary changes and print out new cards.

Pressure-sensitive labels covered with clear label protectors are a quick way to correct spine markings. New call numbers can be typed on labels and used to cover the old ones on catalog cards, pockets, and charge cards, also.

Revisions in your catalog will be done easily if your catalog is in machine-readable form. Your typist can follow your instructions by typing in the new numbers and subject headings and deleting the old. The computer will then rearrange the materials in the database for you. Of course the material itself must still be located and changed to the new classification. If you maintain a print shelf list, you cannot omit changing those cards.

Revising your catalog is a task that requires a block of time, since there are several critical steps involved. Schedule your part of the operation for a time when students are not in the media center and other duties are not pressing. There are staff conference days and holidays during the year when non-instructional personnel are scheduled to work. These are excellent times for your aides or typists to perform their part of the revision.

Failure to check for accuracy when revising your cataloging will cause confusion later should you wish to withdraw materials from your collection; you need all the tracings to pull all cards. An invalid card, left in the catalog, will mislead the user and add time to your withdrawal procedures.

Housing Materials

Max Lerner once was asked to describe in one word the crux of American civilization. He responded, "Access." Access is the key to any plan you devise for shelving materials. Any arrangement in a spacious library media center or in a cramped facility is right if you have held to the principle of accessibility. The arrangement will, and should, change as the demands of your students and staff change. Be flexible and respond to what you see and hear as your collection is used. You may be accused of "fluffing the nest" when you rearrange, but there will be no objections if materials can be located with ease.

- Locations should be designated clearly and attractively, with signs which are professionally prepared if possible. Specific locations should be indicated on catalog cards.

- Designations should be added to catalog cards above the classification. Using pencil to add such notations makes changes easier. If you supervise satellite areas or collections in classrooms you will want to provide access to those materials through your main catalog. If your school has not adopted centralized cataloging of all materials in the building, and items are located in many areas and access not provided to them, this should be a goal of high priority. Materials can be housed wherever use is greatest as long as you have the record of such materials provided through your catalog.

- A ready reference collection near the circulation desk, or near a reference desk if you can staff such a station, will save many steps.

- Oversized books located within the regular collection, possibly on the lowest shelves, are easier to browse and to shelf-read.

- Paperbacks as well as reference books should not be housed near exits, unless they are protected by a security system.

- Vertical files should be located in the main reading area so that students may retrieve them without assistance.

- Periodicals need to be protected, and so, generally speaking, should be housed where retrieved by staff. With the emphasis in the curriculum upon timely information, your periodicals will constitute a very valuable part of your collection.

- Current issues of general periodicals and those popular for leisure reading, as well as the daily newspapers, should not circulate but instead be displayed and available at the circulation desk. I recommend requiring that students sign for these and use them only in the media center. Lest you think restrictions are contrary to the axiom of "access," let me hasten to suggest that your goal should be accessibility to the maximum amount of materials for the greatest number of persons, and a reliable collection of magazines moves you toward that goal.

- Withdrawn issues of newspapers may be offered for students to clip. This will help you to keep the daily papers intact and still permit students to complete that frequent social studies assignment for bringing in a current events article.

- Post a list of all periodical holdings near the indexes. Indicate on this list all back files and their format.

- Microform materials should be housed near the microform readers. Locating these materials and equipment near work stations makes assisting in their use less time-consuming and the supervision less obtrusive.

There was a trend, back at the time of transition from the library of old to the new media center in schools, to shelve audiovisual materials with books. For most of us this proved to be awkward because of the variety of shapes and sizes of audiovisuals. Tampering with materials, because for many pupils they were a novelty in the library, was a problem also. House these audiovisual programs where you can provide the equipment necessary for using them and where they can be retrieved for classroom use.

Finally, prepare guidelines for shelving materials and make them available to your staff assigned this task. Do not leave this to chance. Something could be lost until inventory if improperly shelved!

LIBRARY RESEARCH PLANS

Level I: Pretest of Research Skills

The objective for this library research plan is as follows:

- The students will complete a skills test that will allow the media specialist to determine which locational skills they have mastered

Make copies of Figure 2-1 for the students to see which locational skills they have mastered. Here are the answers to the pretest:

1.	K	9.	O
2.	B	10.	D
3.	A	11.	C
4.	I	12.	E
5.	G	13.	N
6.	L	14.	F
7.	H	15.	P
8.	J	16.	M

After you have corrected the students' pretests, encourage the students to correct any incorrect responses by finding the information in the references listed.

Level II: *Readers' Guide to Periodical Literature*

The following are the objectives for this library research plan:

- The students will review the use of the *Readers' Guide to Periodical Literature* in locating information in magazines.
- The students will understand the format of entries in this index.
- The students will know where to find explanations of the abbreviations used in this index.

- The students will learn about the media center's periodical collection, where it is housed, and the format of back issues.
- The students will learn where to find this index in the media center.
- The students will learn how to request a magazine from the files.
- The students will demonstrate the ability to locate information in this index by completing a brief exercise.

Media Center
Level II
Readers' Guide to Periodical Literature

This lesson is intended as a review of previously acquired skills. Your introduction to the lesson should include this information:

1. *Readers' Guide* is an author-subject index to magazines of non-technical, general interest content.
2. Author and subject entries are arranged in one alphabet.
3. "Suggestions for use" and explanations of the abbreviations are found in the front of each issue.
4. An explanation of the cumulative plan of publication.
5. The location of *Readers' Guide* in your media center.
6. The format of back files, how extensive they are, and how a student may request an issue of a magazine.

Use Figures 2-2 through 2-7 as transparencies or as worksheets. As you discard your semi-monthly and monthly issues of *Readers' Guide* mark them "withdrawn" but save them for use with classes in other skills presentations.

Level III: Developing a Research Proposal

The objectives for this library research plan are as follows:

- The students will read a sample research proposal.
- The students will relate guide questions to the sample proposal.
- The students will use the guide questions to initiate their own proposals.
- The students will prepare a proposal using the answers to the guide questions.
- The students will gain confidence in their ability to organize ideas.
- The students will validate the informational needs associated with their research proposals.

Make copies of Figures 2–8 and 2–9 and distribute them to your students. (NOTE: The sample research proposal on the high cost of movie tickets was prepared by James Nehring of Bethlehem Central High School. It is used with permission.)

RESEARCH SKILLS PRETEST   2–1

Match each item in the left-hand column with the best source of information in the right-hand column.

_____ 1. A book by Danielle Steele   A. *Statistical Almanac of the U.S.*

_____ 2. Brief history of Cambodia   B. *World Book Encyclopedia*

_____ 3. Census figures of the U.S.   C. *Current Biography*

_____ 4. Latitude and longitude of Brussels   D. *Documents of American History*

_____ 5. Winners of the Super Bowl   E. *Masterplots*

_____ 6. Comparisons of compact disc players   F. *Dictionary of Literary Terms*

_____ 7. Birthplace of Margaret Truman   G. *World Almanac*

_____ 8. Date of the New Hampshire primary   H. *Who's Who in America*

_____ 9. A picture of Mona Lisa   I. an atlas

_____ 10. Date of the Monroe Doctrine   J. *New York Times Index*

_____ 11. A picture of Princess Diana   K. the card catalog

_____ 12. Summary of *To Kill a Mockingbird*   L. *Readers' Guide to Periodical Literature*

_____ 13. Chronology of events for the year 1986   M. *Facts on File*

_____ 14. Meaning of ''satire'' in literature   N. *World Book Yearbook*

_____ 15. Review of *Season on the Brink*   O. *Encyclopedia of Art*

_____ 16. Current news summary   P. *Book Review Digest*

IMMIGRATION and emigration

  United States
Don't let them drown: boat people. J. Purnick.
  il NY 12:10-11 Jl 23 '79
Florida's boat people: Haitians. D. Williams
  and others. il Newsweek 93: 37-8 Ap 2 '79
Hanoi's shame—and ours. Nat R 31:956 +
  Ag 3 '79

Readers' Guide to Periodical Literature
CROSS REFERENCE

IMMIGRANTS in the United States

  America: still the promised land il U.S.
   News 87:26-8 Jl 9 '79
    See also
  Aliens
  Chinese in the United States
  Cubans in the United States
  Czechs in the United States

MOTORCYCLE racing

   Don't call it beginner's luck; 125 United
      States Grand Prix. D. Hawkins. il Cycle
      30:78-80+ N '79
        See also
   Drag racing
           Finland
   Last tango in Imatra? J. Greening. Cycle
      30:10+ N '79

           Great Britain
   Silverstone. J. Greening. il Cycle 30:102
      N '79

AFGHANISTAN

   In darkest Afghanistan. P. Theroux. il
      Harper 252:89-90+ Mr '76
        See also
   Villages—Afghanistan
          Foreign relations
             United States
        See United States—Foreign relations—
      Afghanistan

Identify the parts from the following *Readers' Guide* entries and answer the questions below. Record your answers on the "*Readers' Guide* Answer Sheet."

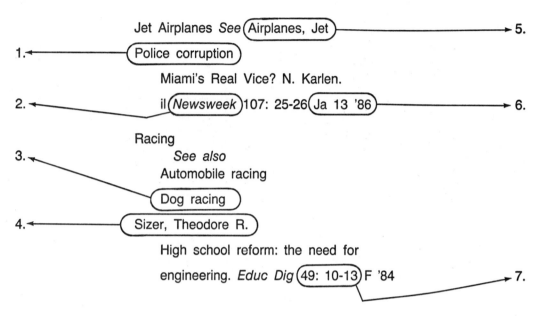

8. The subject headings under which you would find information about racing.

9. What the article "Miami's Real Vice?" is about.

10. The number of years the media center keeps magazines on file.

11. The period of time for which magazines may be checked out.

2–7   *READERS' GUIDE* **ANSWER SHEET**

Use this answer sheet to record your answers to the "*Readers' Guide* Exercise."

1. _____

2. _____

3. _____

4. _____

5. _____

6. _____

7. _____

8. _____

9. _____

10. _____

11. _____

EXTRA CREDIT: Transfer the information from any of the sample entries in the exercise to the request slip below as though you were going to borrow the magazine.

Periodical Request

Periodical _____

Issue _____

Your name _____

Homeroom number _____

Date due _____

GUIDE QUESTIONS FOR RESEARCH PROPOSAL　　2–8

A major problem is encountered frequently by students faced with conducting a research project. It is: "How do I begin?"

The first paragraph of your proposal should answer the following questions:

1. What general topic will my report be about?

2. Why is this topic important?

3. What specific questions will I attempt to answer?

The second paragraph of your proposal should answer this question:

4. How will I go about answering these questions?

The third paragraph of your proposal should answer this question:

5. What answers to my research questions do I expect to find?

Now read the sample proposal. You will see that it was developed to answer the questions listed above.

Using these questions as your guide, you can now develop your own research proposal that will be interesting and well organized.

After your teacher has approved your proposal, you may proceed to gather your information and write your research proposal.

A SAMPLE RESEARCH PROPOSAL:
THE HIGH COST OF MOVIE TICKETS
by Gloria Schnerd　　2–9

I propose to write a paper dealing with the high cost of movie tickets. Clearly this is a topic of concern to any teenager who struggles to earn a little pocket money and expects to be able to afford a few luxuries. Specifically, my paper will attempt to answer the following questions: What is the average cost of a movie ticket these days? What factors make some tickets more expensive than others? How much have ticket prices risen in the last ten years? Why have ticket prices risen? Have ticket prices risen evenly with inflation?

In conducting my research I will read several articles dealing with current trends in the movie industry. I will also read John Enright's *Going to the Movies*, a book that focuses on movie theatre business management. In addition, I plan to conduct interviews with area movie theatre managers. These managers will provide the most up-to-date information, information unavailable in books and magazines.

I expect that my research will show movie ticket prices have risen at a rate faster than inflation during the last ten years. Furthermore, I suspect the reason prices have risen so rapidly is that movie production costs have increased tremendously. I also think that movie managers have become greedier because more people want to go to the movies than ten years ago and are willing to pay the cost. Finally, movie theatres are nicer today than they were ten years ago, and theatre managers have to pay off the loans they took out to upgrade their theatres.

OCTOBER BULLETIN BOARDS

Oktoberfest
United Nations Day
Halloween
Columbus Day
Child Health Day
Canadian Thanksgiving Day
White Cane Safety Day
World Poetry Day
National Day of Prayer
International Red Cross Day
World Food Day

READ . . . Periodically

One suggestion for a bulletin board display for this month of October is entitled: "READ . . . Periodically."

During the first weeks of school, before research assignments are developed, you will observe that students have more free time to read for pleasure. This display will attract their attention to your collection of magazines and news sources. As you familiarize the students with this collection for leisure reading purposes, you will be preparing them also in the locational and retrieval skills they will need for research.

"READ . . . Periodically" should feature as many of your magazines as bulletin board space will accommodate. To prepare this display, you will need:

- Construction paper for a colorful background

- Letters of contrasting color for the title

- Covers from a selection of magazines (use withdrawn issues or photocopies of covers, and include school publications)

- Banners from newspapers in the collection

- Title pages (or photocopies of same) from NewsBank® indexes, *New York Times Current Events on Microfiche, Facts on File*, and other news services

- A list of the titles in your periodical collection

- A list of the public library's holdings

- An example of your periodical request slip

Arrange all materials under the title on your bulletin board. Mount the lists on contrasting paper before adding to the display.

It's Elementary, Mr. Watson

October is a good time to highlight ghost stories, weird tales, and mystery and suspense tales. A bulletin board for the second half of the month could be "It's Elementary, Mr. Watson."

To prepare this bulletin board, you will need:

- A line drawing of a hat, pipe, and magnifying glass
- Construction paper for the background
- Letters of contrasting paper for the caption
- Bibliographies (with annotations) of detective and mystery stories

Bare Bones

Facts on File, Incorporated, distributes a mobile skeleton made of paper that is accompanied by attractive posters and photographs. The mobile kit is called "Bare Bones: Everybody's Inside Out." If you order two kits, you can display both sides of the interesting posters. The skeleton, once assembled, can be mounted against your bulletin board or hung as a mobile.

Attractive titles about anatomy and anthropology from your collection are natural adjuncts to this display. Use black and orange construction paper for the background.

INSERVICE AND PUBLIC RELATIONS: OPERATION OF AUDIOVISUAL EQUIPMENT

Instructional technology is a rapidly changing field. Audiovisual laboratories, computer assisted instruction, and new technologies such as laser discs will continue to offer a variety of instructional methods and tools. As a media specialist, your involvement in the development of new technologies for instructional programs in school will be limited only by your resistance, lack of time, or absence of administrative support.

While striving to become more competent with the newer technologies, our media services are still most in demand where the traditional equipment is concerned.

Now, in October, after a month of providing audiovisual equipment to the staff in your building, you have a good idea of who is proficient with machines and who has difficulty with the simplest mechanisms! At your new-teacher orientation in September, you arranged a time for inservice in equipment operation. You will want to extend an invitation to the rest of the staff because some of the veterans in your building will need the workshop most. Remember the administrators, too.

To those teachers you have identified as consistently showing a lack of skill with the equipment, a personal invitation is in order.

It is difficult to make your inservice sessions mandatory unless your principal offers to do so by relinquishing faculty meeting time. Generally, the number of meetings that can be required of teachers is spelled out by contract.

You will receive the most positive response to your inservice workshops if you can schedule them during the work day, possibily during an activity period or on a conference day.

Your workshop should be composed of two parts:

1. A brief demonstration
2. Open-ended time for hands-on practice with the equipment

The number of sessions you hold will depend upon the variety of equipment your teachers are using.

A few items in your inventory may seem so user friendly that they hardly need your attention. You will be surprised to learn, however, how many of your participants are unfamiliar with the basics of operation as well as the various options many forms of audiovisual equipment offer.

Schedule only a few pieces of equipment for each session in order to allow plenty of time for the participants to try out your directions. Your demonstrations should be brief and basic. If you feel inadequate in your role as "expert," enlist the expertise of your media technician (if you have one) or another faculty member with the requisite skills.

As you plan your demonstrations, prepare a list of "dos and don'ts" for each type of equipment. Tape these technical tips on the machines or in their covers.

A list of general procedures to follow when using equipment should be prepared as a handout. The sample given at the end of this book may be useful for you.

A sample invitation to your workshops is also included with the forms at the end of this book. You will see that you can indicate exactly which types of equipment will be included at each workshop so that teachers can select those sessions in which they are more interested.

Some people needing this inservice will not respond. Indeed, that is an understatement worthy of your attention. Preparing those inservice sessions will be time-consuming, and you will question their worth when attendance is disappointing. However, those who attend will feel good about their new skills, you will have improved your own skills with equipment and as a presenter, and you will have begun to establish your role as a resource person.

November

"No fruits, no flowers, no leaves,
no birds—November!"

Thomas Hood
No!

November Birthdays

1667	Jonathan Swift
1835	Mark Twain
1850	Robert L. Stevenson
1871	Stephen Crane
1879	Vachel Lindsay
1893	John P. Marquand
1898	C. S. Lewis
1900	Margaret Mitchell
1904	Isaac B. Singer
1905	Emlyn Williams
1909	James Agee
1913	Albert Camus
1914	William Gibson
1914	Howard Fast
1917	Jon Cleary
1918	Madeleine L'Engle
1919	Frederik Pohl
1922	Kurk Vonnegut, Jr.
1926	Poul Anderson
1936	Don DeLillo
1939	Margaret Atwood
1952	Robert McKinley

MANAGEMENT TASKS

"While we teach, we learn."

Seneca
Epistolae

The management tasks for the month of November are:

1. Establishing circulation procedures; handling overdues
2. Preparing reserve collections
3. Managing a periodical routing service

Establishing Circulation Procedures; Handling Overdues

Circulation systems vary, even in secondary school media centers, from a very simple pencil and hand-stamp procedure to a fully automated process. Whatever the system of circulation you initiate, it must be based on the policies you establish first.

These policies should reflect the needs of your student body and faculty, should be easy to implement, should have a generous measure of built-in flexibility, and should be developed cooperatively between your staff and those who use your media center. Prior to the evaluation survey, you will conduct with faculty and students in the spring, you may wish to meet with the student governing body or initiate a media center advisory council in order to arrive at student opinion regarding new policies you wish to implement.

Keeping in mind that the flow of materials to and from your media center and the extent that resources are used within your facility are both measures of the effectiveness of your program, you will need to answer such questions as:

1. May all materials be checked out for use outside the media center?
2. May teachers reserve materials for their class use only?
3. Will equipment be loaned, and to whom?
4. How long should loan periods be?
5. May materials be renewed? How often?
6. May people from the community have access to materials and equipment?
7. May teachers borrow materials on "long term"?
8. Should fines be charged for overdues?
9. Should teachers be charged for materials they lose?
10. Should borrowing privileges ever be restricted? If so, under what conditions?

Your answers to these questions (and you can probably add to the list) will be influenced by the size of your collection and your equipment inventory, the reliability of your security, the degree of cooperation among your staff and students, the backing your administration is prepared to offer, the input you receive from students, and the policies that may be in place in your school or district.

Be flexible, but be consistent. Rules waived for one student or teacher should be waived for others. Facilitate use; be chary of restrictions.

In deciding the extent of loan periods you will need to take into consideration both long-term and short-term assignments. Renewals should be encouraged unless the material is requested by someone else.

The availability of a copier in the media center can lessen the demand for use of reference or reserve materials outside of the media center. You could consider offering free copying of brief selections.

Allowing reference books to circulate overnight is a privilege both students and staff appreciate. It makes little sense to have needed materials locked up overnight or on holidays and weekends when they could be in use.

Loaning equipment or materials for community, out-of-school use requires administrative policy and possibly a policy determined district-wide, since it involves the restrictions of insurance coverage.

Before you invoke a policy of charging fines for overdue material, consider whether you want to be responsible for having change on hand, making change, keeping a record of fine monies and banking them, and consistently enforcing the policy. Do fines really teach responsibility?

Once you have developed your circulation policies, post the rules conspicuously and communicate them to students and teachers through the school bulletin, newsletters and, if necessary, at student council meetings and faculty meetings. The faculty must be certain of your circulation policies in order to be supportive of them with their students.

Maintaining control of your media center resources means planning a reliable check-out system and adequate procedures for getting things back from borrowers. Your policies will work if your procedures have credibility. Students and teachers will lose confidence in a system that is fraught with errors. When you consider automating media center procedures, circulation should head the list.

Anyone assigned to circulation desk duties should make certain that:

- the student's signature is legible
- homeroom, or in-school address, is given
- date due slip is stamped
- circulation card is stamped

Good charging systems are around that will automate just this part of your circulation procedure. Most systems require the use of a check-out card, personalized for each student. Students will misplace or forget these cards, so it is advisable to keep them on file at the desk. A rotary file is handy for this purpose.

At the end of each day, your circulation should be recorded and the charge cards filed by due date. Reference and reserve cards should be separate since they will require more immediate action. A very desirable feature of the automated circulation systems is their potential for keeping all circulation records, including spread sheets that will indicate the figures for a particular type of media, and the totals by day, week, month, and year.

Prepare instructions for checking in materials that include these:

- Retrieve the charge card from the circulation file

- Match accession numbers
- Cross out the borrower's name; replace card in material
- Cross out the date on the date due slip
- Organize periodicals alphabetically by title for filing
- Organize books and audiovisuals by call number for shelving

If your circulation system is an automated one, you can add or delete overdue materials daily, print out overdue notices as frequently as you wish, prepare homeroom lists of students with overdue materials, and generate a list of names for suspension of privileges if that is your policy. Adding the word processing function and a mail merge feature to your system would allow you to write letters home to parents as necessary.

Without these data processing capabilities, you need to organize and complete these tasks as efficiently and as accurately as possible.

If you wish to send out multiple, sequential notices to students and staff, you may consider buying multi-copy pads of overdue notices from a supplier. The notice is written once, the first copy torn off and sent out. You can than attach the remaining notices to the charge card in your circulation file. If the material is returned, the duplicate notices are destroyed when the material is discharged. If it is not returned, the additional notices can be sent out sequentially.

Observe whether duplicate notices make any difference in the rate of returns. They may not, in which case you may decide to send one notice only and implement other follow-up procedures.

Several forms for retrieving material are included in this book for your use.

Failure to return material, after due notification, leaves you little choice but to impose penalties of some kind. Since your object is to teach responsibility and a concern for sharing resources with the rest of the schoool, your first step should be a personal contact with the student. Letters to parents, assigning detention, restricting borrowing privileges, and eliciting the help of the principal are all possibilities for further action. Be sure before taking such action that your overdue messages have actually reached the student and also double-check your records to verify that no error has been made, that the material has not somehow gotten misplaced or re-shelved. If the student appears to have a chronic problem with returning borrowed materials on time you may want to talk with his or her counselor. There may be something going on which precludes attention to media center rules. Be sympathetic.

You may find that students withdraw from school carrying media center materials with them! (Brown bags of books mysteriously appear from time to time!) Ask your principal and the guidance office to cooperate with your procedures by requiring the media specialist's signature on the withdrawal form along with the signatures of the student's teachers.

Your principal may allow the withholding of report cards at marking time for students who have not returned materials. To some, this is an effective incentive to return materials. Unfortunately, to others, it is an invitation to remain delinquent!

Preparing Reserve Collections

The need for reserve collections of materials may arise for a number of different reasons:

- A teacher may make an assignment that calls for specific, limited materials.
- You and the teacher may decide that an assignment should be completed in the media center.
- You may want to focus attention upon a particular topic to stimulate interest in the materials.
- You may have a group of materials that are too valuable to circulate (such as a personal collection on loan, or materials obtained through interlibrary loan).

If you decide to establish a reserve collection, your procedures should allow control of these materials, should designate the collection clearly and make it accessible, and should permit use to be recorded in your statistics.

To establish control, determine how long the materials are to be on reserve, whether they are to be used in the media center only, and, if they are to circulate, what the borrowing period is to be:

1. Select the materials and gather them on a book cart.
2. Remove the book cards.
3. Write "reserve" on the date due slip.
4. Duplicate the book card information on a reserve card. Reserve cards can be purchased from supply companies, or you can print your own.
5. Indicate on the reserve card whether the material may be taken from the media center or whether it is restricted to "media center only" use.
6. Arrange the book cards by classification and file them at the circulation desk behind a divider that designates reserve.
7. If the materials are for media center use only, count them once for the circulation record. If you control use with signatures on the reserve card, you may count use for each day's circulation.

Should you decide to leave the regular book card in the material, you will want to indicate its reserve status in some way so that it does not get re-shelved in the regular collection. Plastic or metal signals, or "flags," can be purchased for this purpose. Slip one on each book card as you prepare the materials for reserve. Paper clips serve this purpose inexpensively.

If you anticipate using a particular reserve collection again it is helpful to have a bibliography of the materials selected. While you have the book cards pulled from the materials your typist can prepare the bibliography from them. If you have a computer, consider the programs that have been written specifically for composing bibliographies.

Keep the reserve cards intact for any reserve collections you are likely to prepare again next semester, or next year. As new materials are acquired that are appropriate for established reserve collections, prepare a reserve card as you process the material and keep it with the others. Ask your typist to add the title to the bibliography that is on disk or in print. Updating a bibliography that has been computer-generated is easy since the entries can be made randomly and the computer will re-sort the entries when you print out a new hard copy.

Whether requested by a teacher or not, any time you prepare a collection for a particular unit of study it is wise to alert the staff at the public library. Your students may deplete the public library's titles on the subject unless they are notified in time to place them on reserve also.

Managing a Periodical Routing Service

With the proliferation of new magazines and their increasing costs, the personal acquisition of titles is becoming more difficult for most educators. At the same time, it is more critical each year for teachers to be well-informed and aware of global developments and concerns, the advent of new technologies, educational trends, and changes in their own curricula. Additionally, they are, as others in the society, more interested in leisure pursuits, intellectual stimulation, and their own personal growth.

For these reasons, a periodical routing service from the media center collection will be popular.

First, you will need to duplicate enough copies of your list of periodical holdings to distribute to each member of the staff. Include the non-instructional staff and the administrators.

A memo about a periodical routing service is included in the Appendix for your consideration. When you have received the responses to your memo, follow this procedure for setting up your services:

1. Print or type the name of the magazine at the top of the index card.
2. Add the names of the persons requesting that magazine.
3. Indicate whether the magazine or the table of contents is desired.
4. Alphabetize the cards and create a file for them.
5. When new issues of the magazine arrive:
   a. Fill out the routing slips.
   b. Staple the slips to the magazines.
   c. Complete a charge card or slip for the magazine and file in the day's circulation.
   d. As the magazines are returned, add new names to the routing slips and charge them out to those persons.
   e. If the request is for table of contents only, copy the appropriate page of the magazine and route it.

LIBRARY RESEARCH PLANS

Level I: Almanacs

The objectives for this library research plan are as follows:

- The students will locate the almanacs in the media center.
- The students will find specific information in an almanac, using the table of contents and the index.
- The students will complete a social studies assignment that requires the location of current facts about a country.
- The students will explore the differences between two almanacs: *World Almanac* and *Information Please Almanac*.

- The students will read the prepared guide and complete the accompanying exercise before starting the assignment.
- The students will use a prepared outline to organize their information.
- The students will write a brief report based on their research in the almanacs.
- The students will use topic sentences in their writing.

Make copies of Figures 3–1 through 3–3 and distribute them to your students. Here are the answers to Figure 3–2:

1. World
2. Information Please
3. World
4. Information Please
5. World
6. 496,222 square miles
7. three
8. Wolverine
9. Los Angeles Raiders
10. Information Please

Level II: Research Skills Pretest

The objective for this library research plan is as follows:

- The students will complete a worksheet that will assist the media specialist in evaluating their mastery of locational skills.

Makes copies of Figures 3–4 and 3–5, and distribute these to your students.

Level III: Renaissance Research

The objectives for this library research plan are as follows:

- The students will use general and specific biographic references to research a person from the Renaissance.
- The students will use proper names as subject entries to the card catalog.
- The students will consider the influence of an individual in the context of history.
- The students will use the skill of notetaking to prepare a short research paper.
- The students will prepare a bibliography using correct bibliographic form.

Make copies of Figures 3-6 and 3-7, and distribute them to your students.

3–1   **GUIDE TO ALMANACS**

Almanacs contain a wealth of basic information about almost any subject. They are a particularly good source of up-to-date statistical information about people, business, sports, countries, and world events. Most data in almanacs is revised annually.

The two almanacs you will use for this assignment are general almanacs, covering many topics:

- *World Almanac*

- *Information Please Almanac*

Each of these includes information about important historical events pertaining to your assigned country as well as events of the past year.

It is important to use the indexes and tables of contents to locate information about any subject. Your teacher may suggest that you complete the skills exercise before starting your social studies assignment.

The almanacs in your media center are located ————————————————————————

——— .

Locate the latest edition of each almanac.

Name _____   Class _____

Date _____

ALMANACS EXERCISE 3–2

Answer the following questions:

1. Which almanac includes its comprehensive index in the front of the book?

   _____

2. Which almanac includes a table of contents as well as a comprehensive index?

   _____

3. Which almanac includes a "Quick Reference Index" at the back?

   _____

4. Which almanac contains a "Writer's Guide"?

   _____

5. Which almanac contains noted writers' birthdates?

   _____

6. What is the area of Peru in square miles?

   _____

7. How many colors are on the Belgium flag?

   _____

8. What is the nickname for the state of Michigan?

   _____

9. Which football team won the Super Bowl in 1984?

   _____

10. Which almanac contains a bibliography of additional references on many topics?

   _____

3–3   **COUNTRY RESEARCH**

The country you have been assigned is _____ .
The reference books you will use are the latest editions of *World Almanac* and *Information Please Almanac*. You will locate the following information about your country:

Geography
    1. Location
    2. Neighboring nations or bodies of water
    3. Principal rivers and mountains
    4. Largest city

Government
    1. Capital city
    2. Current leaders and their titles
    3. Type of government
    4. Alliances with other governments

People
    1. Total population
       a. Density
       b. Ethnic groups
       c. Life expectancy
    2. Principal languages
    3. Literacy level
    4. Major religions

Resources
    1. Major agricultural products
    2. Other natural resources

Industrial Development
    1. Gross national product
    2. Major exports
    3. Major imports
    4. Unemployment rate

History
    1. One important historical event pre-1900
    2. One important historical event post-1900

Using the information you have gathered, you are to write a report about your country consisting of six paragraphs. The six paragraphs will present information on the six topics outlined above.
Write in complete sentences. Introduce each paragraph with a topic sentence.

Your report is due _____ .

Name _____ Class _____

Date _____

3–4   **RESEARCH SKILLS PRETEST**

Record your answers to this pretest on the answer sheet.

1. Choose one of the following subjects:

   Watergate   Criminal behavior
   Automobile repair   the rock star, Sting
   Lions   Painting
   Ballet   Metropolitan Museum of Art
   Castles   Women as engineers
   Cross country skiing   Nostradamus
   Dreams   National holidays
   Stephen King   United Nations
   Olympic gymnastics   Madrigals

   Your own topic _____

2. List five specific sources of information about your subject that may be found in the media center collection of print and nonprint materials:

   a. One of these sources must be in nonprint format (microfiche, audiovisual program, or computer program will qualify).

   b. One of the five sources must be a magazine article.

   c. One of the five sources must be a reference book.

3. Give two subheadings or cross-references you came upon in your research that would allow you to narrow down your topic.

4. If you were to write about the subject you chose, what would be the actual title of your paper?

Name _____   Class _____

Date _____

PRETEST ANSWER SHEET   3–5

1. Subject chosen: _____

2. Five sources of information—include call numbers, author or title entries, and specific citations for magazine articles:

   _____

   _____

   _____

   _____

   _____

   _____

   _____

   _____

   _____

   _____

   _____

3. Suggested subheadings or references that would narrow down your chosen topic:

   a. _____

   b. _____

4. Title of your paper:

   _____

   _____

Name _____ Class _____

Date _____

RENAISSANCE RESEARCH ASSIGNMENT

You will be assigned one of the Renaissance personalities below. You are to research that person using the resources in the library and write a two- to three-page paper describing that person's life and contributions to the Renaissance. Plan on using at least two sources for your information. You must also include a bibliography.

ART

Michelangelo
da Vinci
Raphael
El Greco
Cellini
Holbein

Rembrandt
Giotto
Titian
Durer
Breughel

LITERATURE

Cervantes
Machiavelli
Chaucer
Shakespeare

SCIENCE

Copernicus
Newton
Vesalius
Galileo
Harvey

MUSIC

Palestrina

PATRONS

Lorenzo de' Medici

You will research and write about:

_____

Name _____   Class _____

Date _____

3–7   **GUIDE TO RENAISSANCE RESEARCH ASSIGNMENT**

Your assignment calls for you to research the Renaissance period of history, first by learning something about a person who lived at that time, and then about that person's influence on that period of history.

1. Be prepared with index cards for taking notes as you research your topic. Each time you use a source, you should write down the bibliographic information for use later in your bibliography. (Ask your media specialist for a style sheet showing correct bibliographic form.)

2. You will need to know the full name of the person you have been assigned and how that name appears in indexes. The following general biographical references, which contain brief entries, will help you get started:

Call Number   *Title*

_____   *Webster's Biographical Dictionary*

_____   *The Reader's Encyclopedia*

_____   master index to any general encyclopedia

_____   _____

3. For more information about the person, use the card catalog for other sources. Use the person's name as a subject.

4. Other entries to the card catalog to look for are:

Art—History
Renaissance
Europe—History

5. Write your paper from your notes.

NOVEMBER BULLETIN BOARDS

Sojourner Truth Day
Veterans' Day
American Education Week
Thanksgiving Day
American Music Week
Election Day
Author Day
UNESCO Anniversary
Guy Fawkes Day
Dunce Day
Sadie Hawkins Day
Book Week
Canadian Remembrance Day

Have You Checked Our References?

Unless students have done research in your media center, they may think of "references" as encyclopedias and almanacs only.

A bulletin board highlighting your many references will be timely in November when students will be starting papers, becoming interested in national sports events, and settling into their studies.

You can find material for the "Have You Checked Our References?" display by searching through your publishers' catalogs and flyers. Many publishers include attractive posters of new materials. Cut out pictures and titles of the references in your collection. The covers of withdrawn issues of such titles as *Current Biography* can be used; you might choose a picture of a popular figure. Include withdrawn indexes to news services, such as *Facts on File*. Book jackets can be duplicated on a copier for display. If there are particular references you want to include about which you can find no printed material, copy the title page or an interesting page from the book. Identify the resource with a felt-tip pen. If possible, include references from many different subject areas.

The materials you'll need for this display are:

- Orange construction paper to cover the board

- 3″ or 4″ letters cut from brown paper

- Brown construction paper for mounting small articles

- Posters

- Clippings from publishers' catalogs/flyers

- Withdrawn indexes or issues of serial references

I'm Thankful For . . .

A Thanksgiving theme lends itself to the same color scheme of orange and brown later in the month of November. Your title can be "I'm Thankful For . . ." and you'll need:

- Orange construction paper for the background
- Brown and gold paper for limbs and leaves (or limbs from shrubs or vines)

On the orange background, construct a "tree" with bare limbs. These can either be actual small, flexible branches or vines, or paper branches.

Cut three or four dozen leaves from brown and gold paper. Start your Thanksgiving tree by printing several leaves with appropriate endings to the phrase "I'm thankful for . . ." Use a stapler to add the leaves to your branches. You may suggest student participation and keep the leaves at the desk. The "tree" can then grow during the week or two you have the display mounted.

INSERVICE AND PUBLIC RELATIONS: LIAISON WITH DEPARTMENTS

If your faculty is small in number or if there are no department heads or supervisors in the school management organization, your methods of communication with staff can and should be simple and direct. A walk down the hall to see a teacher, a note in a teacher's school mailbox, or a notice on the faculty room bulletin board will suffice.

Such methods always may prove adequate and useful for some purposes, but with large numbers of teachers to serve there is a need to establish liaison with department heads.

Titles for these persons differ from district to district. There may be "supervisors," "department heads," or even "section leaders" in the organizational hierarchy of your school. These persons are important to you in your support services, and you will want to become an important team member to them. They are the authorities regarding the curriculum and what the educational goals are for their departments. They are in the best position to know what materials are needed to support educational goals, what new courses are being planned or which ones may be deleted, and what their staff's needs are in terms of media.

You can be an important source of information for them, you can provide them with options and choices, you can locate the best resources at the best cost, and you can provide a learning center where their teachers can find enrichment activities and materials.

From supervisors, you need:

- Information to assist you in preparing a budget
- Support for your policies and procedures
- Evaluation of the effectiveness of your services
- Recommendations for purchases
- Communication from you to departmental staff
- Preview of possible purchases

If the number of media specialists on your staff is more than yourself, divide the assignments for departmental liaison between or among yourselves. Include all departments, regardless of their size. These assignments will be most effective if they are made with individuals' preferences or educational background in mind.

The kinds of information you will want to convey to the supervisors are:

- New acquisitions of interest to their departments
- Procedures regarding class use of the media center
- New services you are initiating
- Announcements of inservice programs

During November, you should request an invitation to department meetings. You can suggest that if time permits, you would like to show the staff some of the new materials you have received. Distribute order cards at the meeting and indicate your desire to receive suggestions for purchase from the staff. You will learn a great deal in these meetings simply by listening to the discussion of topics related to curriculum and teaching strategies. Most supervisors will be happy to have you attend their meetings regularly, but your responsibilities to several departments may make this impossible. You can ask at least that the agendas and minutes be routed to you.

As you read book reviews, software reviews, or articles of interest to teachers, copy them and send them to the appropriate supervisors for routing to their staff.

Begin this month to discuss with supervisors what their suggestions might be for improvement of collection or services, since you, as well as they, will be preparing next year's budget within the next few weeks.

After a teacher has brought a class into the media center for research, drop a note to the supervisor telling him or her how successful the activity was. A copy to the teacher involved will be appreciated, also. This procedure helps the supervisor to stay informed about media center activities, provides positive information about the learning climate of the school, and lets the teachers know you want to be a partner in the educational process.

December

December Birthdays

1775   Jane Austen
1857   Joseph Conrad
1865   Joseph Rudyard Kipling
1870   Saki
1873   Willa Cather
1892   Rebecca West
1894   James Thurber
1903   Erskine Caldwell
1905   Dalton Trumbo
1912   Jay Bennett
1917   Arthur C. Clarke
1919   Shirley Jackson
1924   Rod Serling
1928   Philip K. Dick
1934   Joan Didion
1949   Mary Gordon

MANAGEMENT TASKS

"Work without Hope draws nectar in a sieve,
and Hope without an object cannot live."

Samuel Taylor Coleridge
Work Without Hope

The management tasks for December, that brief, hectic, happy month in the school year, are:

1. Preparing the budget
2. Preparing for holiday break

Preparing the Budget

Fiscal considerations are critically important in our jobs as secondary school media specialists. We are the ones responsible for developing a sound budget, and we are held accountable for the allocations and expenditures of those funds. It is quite possible your media program budget will require supervision of an amount of money much greater than any other departments in the school. This is appropriate, since the services you administer affect all other departments. This is one of the reasons your lines of communication, the liaison patterns you establish with the other departments in the school, are so important. You cannot develop a successful budget in isolation. You need to be in touch with the supervisors, the total educational program, other teachers, and your own media staff.

If you are in a new position as a secondary school media specialist you will have inherited a budget within which you must work. Perhaps it is one which serves you well, and if that is so you may pattern the next year's budget in a similar manner. Now, during December, is your opportunity to construct a budget which will reflect your goals for your media program.

There are many different patterns in schools for setting department budgets. In a near ideal case you may be asked to submit a program budget which will analyze for your principal what you want to do and how much money it will take for you to accomplish your goals. It would then logically follow that if your goals are accepted and your estimates of needed funds are reasonably accurate, the budget would be approved.

It is more likely that an amount of money which the district administrators feel will be acceptable to the community will be decided upon, the individual buildings in the district will receive "per pupil" allotments, and from that amount your principal will apportion amounts to the various categories of the total school program.

In this latter situation, your principal will notify you of the total amount of money he or she has allocated to the media program. Working with that amount, you may then be asked to decide how your budget is to be spent. It is also possible your principal may make those decisions for you. If this is the case, you will have little control over your budget, but certainly less work.

By the end of the school year, you will have specific recommendations regarding the manner in which the budget process is handled for you. Your annual report will be an appropriate place to present this issue.

Prepare a summary of the items you will include in your budget. Categories for expenditures ordinarily will include:

- Equipment
- Supplies
- Audiovisual materials
- Books
- Periodicals
- Membership dues
- Equipment leasing
- Film/video rental
- Bookbinding
- Service and repair contracts
- Student help
- Conference and travel

Equipment is often purchased at the district or building level from funds outside the media center budget. Your part in the determination of these purchases may be advisory since expensive items are generally placed on bid. You can help in this process by obtaining prices from vendors and by preparing specifications for models which you know will best serve your needs. Vendors' catalogs, looking at equipment at conferences, and becoming familiar with the repair records of equipment in your inventory will help you to become knowledgeable about equipment models. Vendors are often willing to bring pieces of equipmemt into your media center for demonstration, and even to leave for trial use, if they know you are interested in purchasing.

It is not productive to be too frugal when allocating money for office supplies. You need the right amount and kind of tools and supplies to keep your office running smoothly.

Maintenance contracts on office equipment are expensive but important. Single calls to fix typewriters, copiers, or computers are much more expensive in the long run and it is difficult to predict need so many months before the budget goes into effect. Often your equipment will be covered by group contracts for the building or the district. If you are expected to budget for the repair of all audiovisual equipment in the media center you will need to locate a service company that can repair all kinds and with the best hourly fee you can negotiate. Generally this is handled by the district business administrator, but do not leave this item to chance.

Your professional organization dues are not an appropriate item in your budget, but you may want to earmark funds for institutional membership in the local educational television station or arts council, student support groups, or district-wide service organizations.

If you have had difficulty enlisting student help for library duties or audiovisual deliveries you may want to consider a line item in your budget for paying student employees.

Look ahead to media-related and other professional conferences that you feel would be beneficial for yourself or other members of your staff. Include plans for your non-instructional staff to attend workshops pertaining to their duties.

The figures you submit in your budget summary should represent as closely as possible the actual expenditures you anticipate. Most school business procedures allow for some transfers of funds from one budget code to another during the school year, but sound decisions now will produce a budget you can live with in the coming year.

Be parpared to justify your budget summary.

Preparing for Holiday Break

Set aside time in early December to inspect the media center and to prepare work orders and maintenance requests. The non-instructional staff will work when school is not in session, and this is a fine time to get necessary repairs done. Check study carrels and other furniture to see if graffiti must be removed (graffiti begets graffiti). Pencil sharpeners should be intact, shelving may need re-alignment, work areas may need to be re-arranged. The installation of electrical outlets, lights, alarms, bulletin boards; the cleaning of floors and carpets; these are all jobs that must be done when your center is not open. It is up to you to bring maintenance projects to the principal's attention. You will be competing with others for maintenance crew time, so you may want to submit your requests in priority order.

A few of the tasks you can assign your clerical staff during the holiday break are:

- Verification of equipment location
- Repair-check of equipment
- Completion of processing of materials
- Preparation of bibliographies
- Filing of catalog cards
- Withdrawal of cards from catalog

LIBRARY RESEARCH PLANS

Level I: Applied Science

The objectives for this library research are as follows:

- The students will locate specific information on a topic in the media center.
- The students will complete a fact sheet about their topics.
- The students will cite the sources where they located information.
- The students will write paragraphs summarizing the information they located.
- The students will enter this paragraph of information into a computer.
- The students will gain experience following both verbal and written directions.

Make copies of Figures 4-1 and 4-2, and distribute them to your students. Your students will need access to a word processor computer program and computer.

Level II: The Victorian Age

The objectives for this library research plan are as follows:

- The students will use specific reference books in the media center.

- The students will learn the location of reference books in the media center.
- The students will locate information about a writer of the Victorian period.
- The students will locate biographical information, quotations, poetry, and prose writings by the assigned authors using the card catalog, a book of quotations, and an index to poetry.
- The students will recite selections from the Victorian writers in front of the class.
- The students will take notes and share their information with classmates.

You will need copies of Figures 4–3 through 4–13. Figures 4–5 through 4–13 are illustrations of various card catalog cards and available reference books.

Level III: Charles Dickens and the Victorian Age

The objectives for this library research plan are as follows:

- The students will use reference books to locate specific information about the Victorian Age.
- The students will prepare a timeline that will present the relationship of important events of the age.
- The students will complete a research project that will be shared with classmates in a Dickens festival.

Make copies of Figures 4–14 through 4–16, and distribute them to your students.

(*Note*: The research proposal on Dickens and the Victorian Age was written by James Yeara. It is used with permission.)

4–1   **GUIDE TO APPLIED SCIENCE RESEARCH**

To complete your science assignment on a breed of domestic animal, you will use general encyclopedias and specific science references. First locate the index in the encyclopedia you are using. Some general encyclopedias have a master index volume; others have an index in each volume.

The indexes in other reference books are also the keys to the information contained in those volumes. Some of the books you should use are:

_____

_____

_____

_____

_____

These references are located _____

_____

Remember to tell which books you used in the area provided on your worksheet. Your report should be brief, but should include the important facts. Here is an example.

The Thoroughbred Horse

There is a breed of horse that is used in most countries for saddle racing. It was first bred in England, but is now found in many countries around the world. The thoroughbred horse has a straight back and large chest, but a small head. The bones in its legs are short, which gives the horse its ability to take long, fast strides. The thoroughbred horse is generally a bay or chestnut color.

Name _____   Class _____

Date _____

APPLIED SCIENCE WORKSHEET: BREEDS   4–2

In the media center, research the breed you have chosen: Kind of animal (sheep, horse,

etc.) _____

Breed _____

   1. Characteristics:

      a. Color(s) _____

      b. Size _____

      c. Other features _____

          _____

   2. What is it noted for (work, meat, eggs, etc.)? _____

      _____

   3. Where did this breed originate? _____

   4. Is it popular in our country? Why or why not? _____

      _____

      _____

   5. Production figures: _____

   6. Additional information: _____

      _____

   7. References (at least two):

      a. Title _____

          _____

          Author _____

          Date of publication _____ Pages _____

      b. Title _____

          _____

          Author _____

          Date of publication _____ Pages _____

   8. Write your one-paragraph report on the back of this sheet.

   9. Ask your librarian for instructions for the _____

      word processing program for entering your report into the computer.

4–3 INSTRUCTIONS FOR THE VICTORIAN AGE RESEARCH

You will be assigned one writer of the Victorian Age. You are to find:

- His or her dates of birth and death
- Titles of his or her most famous works
- Reasons for this person's importance

Where it is noted, a copy of a poem or a selection of prose will be required and recitation of the same.

Put all your information on a 3″ × 5″ card to be shared with classmates.

Writers of the Victorian Age

1. Thomas Babington Macaulay (plus a famous quotation)
2. Elizabeth Barrett (plus her poem ''The Cry of Children'')
3. Charles Darwin (plus a famous quotation)
4. Thomas Hardy (plus either the poem ''The Darling Thrush'' or ''Neutral Tones'')
5. Alfred, Lord Tennyson (plus the poem ''Ulysses'')
6. John Keats (plus a poem of your choice)
7. Dante Gabriel Rossetti (plus a poem of your choice)
8. Robert Browning (plus a poem of your choice)
9. John Stuart Mill (plus a famous quotation)
10. William Thackeray
11. Lewis Carroll (plus a selection to recite)
12. Anthony Trollope
13. Anne Brontë
14. Charlotte Brontë
15. Emily Brontë
16. John Ruskin (plus a famous quotation)
17. Matthew Arnold (plus the poem ''Dover Beach'')
18. Gerard Manley Hopkins (plus the poem ''Spring and Fall'')
19. Sir Walter Scott
20. George Eliot

Name _____   Class _____

Date _____

GUIDE TO THE VICTORIAN AGE   4–4

The following titles are a few of the reference books that you will use to complete your assignment on writers of the Victorian Age:

Call Number	Title
_____	*The Reader's Encyclopedia*
_____	*The Encyclopedia of World Biography*
_____	*British Authors of the Nineteenth Century*
_____	*Webster's Biographical Dictionary*
_____	*Granger's Index to Poetry*
_____	*Bartlett's Familiar Quotations*
_____	_____

These references are located _____ .

Your selected writer of the Victorian Age is:

_____

```
F     Carroll, Lewis
CAR     The annotated Alice; Alice's adventures
      in Wonderland & Through the looking
      glass; illus by John Tenniel; with an
      introd and notes by Martin Gardner.
      Potter [c1960]
      352p illus

      A scholarly analysis is presented of
      Carroll's use of mathematics, riddles,
      and jokes along with the text of his 2
      great books about Alice.  Bibliog

      1 Fantasies  I Ed  II T  III T: Alice's
      adventures in Wonderland  IV T: Through
      the looking glass


02868       04      633506      © THE BAKER & TAYLOR CO.
```

HARDY, THOMAS

823
HAW

Hawkins, Desmond
   Hardy: novelist and poet. Barnes &
Noble [c1976]
247p illus

A chronological investigation of
Hardy's life and voluminous output as
a novelist and poet combines biographical and historical material with in-
terpretive critical assessments of individual writings. Bibliog

   1 Hardy, Thomas   I T

ISBN 0-06-492752-0

02720   16   460585   ҫ THE BAKER & TAYLOR CO   7102

```
                    TROLLOPE, ANTHONY

921         Snow, Charles Percy, Baron Snow
TROL           Trollope: his life and art, by C. P.
LOPE        Snow.  Scribner [c1975]
            191p illus (part col)

            Profiles the nineteenth-century En-
            glish novelist paying particular at-
            tention to his unhappy childhood and
            years as a successful businessman.
            Bibliog




            1 Trollope, Anthony


02173       01      438045      © THE BAKER & TAYLOR CO.    6026
```

William Rose Benét

THE READER'S ENCYCLOPEDIA

SECOND EDITION

THOMAS Y. CROWELL COMPANY

New York / Established 1834

violating Tennessee law by teaching evolution in a public school. (See SCOPES TRIAL.) Although Darrow lost the case, he destroyed the reputation of the prosecuting attorney, William Jennings Bryan.

Darrow wrote two novels, *Farmington* (1904) and *An Eye for an Eye* (1905). Among his other volumes are *Crime: Its Cause and Its Treatment* (1922); *Infidels and Heretics* (with Wallace Rice, 1929), an anthology; and *The Story of My Life* (1932). He appears as a character in *Inherit the Wind* (1955), a play based on the Scopes trial, by Robert E. Lee and Jerome Lawrence, and in Meyer Levin's book *Compulsion* (1956), based on the Loeb-Leopold case.

D'Artagnan. See Charles de Baatz d'ARTAGNAN.

Darwin, Charles Robert (1809–1882). English naturalist, grandson of Erasmus DARWIN. An original expounder of the theory of evolution by natural selection, since known as Darwinism, he was to have a profound influence on human concepts of life and the universe. Although he studied medicine at Edinburgh and prepared for the ministry at Cambridge, his abiding interest was natural history, and it was as naturalist that he sailed on the *Beagle* (1831–1836) on an expedition to southern islands, South American coasts, and Australia. On his return to England he published *Zoology of the Voyage of the Beagle* (1840). As secretary of the Geological Society (1838–1841), he came into contact with the noted geologist Sir Charles Lyell (1797–1875), who urged him to write on his experiments in inbreeding and his theory of evolution by natural selection. He received (1858) from Alfred Russel Wallace (1823–1913) an abstract outlining an identical theory of natural selection, independently arrived at. He published Wallace's essay along with his own, written in 1844, in 1858. In 1859 he published his ORIGIN OF SPECIES; it is said that the first edition sold out in one day, and immediately a raging controversy arose. Within one year, the book's importance, still felt today, as the leading work in natural philosophy in the history of mankind, was recognized. Darwin's later important works include *The Movements and Habits of Climbing Plants* (1865), *The Variation of Animals and Plants under Domestication* (1868), *The Descent of Man* (1871), and *Selection in Relation to Sex* (1871). See SCOPES TRIAL.

Darwin, Erasmus (1731–1802). English physician, botanist, and poet. He is the author of *The Botanic Garden* (1789, 1791), a didactic poem in heroic couplets discoursing on plants and flowers according to the theories of Linnaeus. Darwin's *Zoönomia* (1794–1796) is a treatise on evolutionary development, not, however, in the sense that his grandson Charles Robert DARWIN was to assign to that term.

Das, Deb Kumar (1936–   ). Indian poet writing in English; also a research scientist. He published *The Night Before Us* (1960).

Dasharatha. In Hindu legend, a king of the solar dynasty; in the Ramayana, father of Rama. He had three chief queens, and when the sage Rishyasringa performed a special sacrifice for him, Rama was born to Kaushalya, Lakshmana and Shatrughna to Srmitra, and Bharata to Kaikeyi. His daughter was Shanta. After he ordered Rama into fourteen years' exile in order to keep a promise he had made to the evil-minded Kaikeyi, he died of a broken heart.

Dashwood, Elinor and Marianne. See SENSE AND SENSIBILITY.

Dashwood, Elizabeth Monica. See E. M. DELAFIELD.

Datta, Sudhindranath (1901–1960). Indian poet and critic in Bengali. He was a leader of the modernist movement in Bengali and translated European poetry. His best-known work is *Orchestra*.

Daudet, Alphonse (1840–1897). French novelist of the naturalist school. Daudet is noted for his keen observation, his sympathetic portrayal of character, and his vivid presentation of incident. His novels deal with life in Provence, his birthplace, and with the various social classes of Paris. The Provençal stories (see TARTARIN), vigorous and good-humored, include LETTRES DE MON MOULIN, *Tartarin de Tarascon* (1872); *Tartarin sur les Alpes* (1885), and *Port-Tarascon* (1890). Daudet's novels of Parisian manners include *Le Nabob* (1877), NUMA ROUMESTAN, *Les Rois en exil* (1879), and *Sapho* (1884).

Daudet, Léon (1868–1942). French journalist and writer. The son of Alphonse Daudet, he gave up medicine to devote himself to political journalism. His intemperate, antidemocratic articles, polemical essays, and diatribes at first appeared in *Le Gaulois, Le Figaro,* and the fanatically anti-Semitic *La Libre Parole;* then, in 1908, Daudet became coeditor with Charles Maurras of the ultraroyalist Catholic journal L'ACTION FRANÇAISE. For 20 years the force of his invective was feared, and he wielded a political influence that enabled him to be elected to the Chamber of Deputies, where he served from 1919 to 1924. His influence was, however, insufficient to sustain a murder charge which he had brought against the chauffeur in whose cab his son had committed suicide. The chauffeur prosecuted him, and, following a noisy trial, he was sentenced to prison for defamation. With royalist help he escaped and fled to Belgium in 1927. Daudet wrote the novels *L'Astre noir* (*The Black Heavenly Body,* 1893), *Les Morticoles* (1894), and *Sylla et son destin* (1922). His nonfiction books include *L'Avant-guerre* (1913), *Souvenirs* (1914), *L'Hérédo* (1916), *Le Monde des images* (1919), and *Le Stupide XIX*ᵉ *siècle* (*The Stupid XIXth Century,* 1922).

Daumier, Honoré (1808–1879). French painter and caricaturist. On the staff of *La Caricature* and *Charivari,* he produced an enormous number of powerful lithographs commenting with bitter humor, scathing satire, or tragic seriousness upon the faults of the bourgeoisie, the corruption of the law, and the injustices of his age. His direct, economically stated paintings with their superb handling of light and shade remained unappreciated until after his death.

Dauphin. The heir to the French crown under the Valois and Bourbon dynasties. Guy VIII, count of Vienne, was the first so styled, apparently because he wore as his emblem a dolphin. The title descended in the family until 1349, when Humbert III ceded his *seigneurie,* the Dauphiné, to Philippe VI (du Valois), one condition being that the heir of France assume the title of *le Dauphin.* The first French prince so called was Jean, who succeeded Philippe; the last was a Duc d'Angoulême, son of Charles X, who renounced the title in 1830. The

Two roads diverged in a yellow wood. The Road Not Taken. Robert Frost. HelP; NoAM; RFM; SoSe; VoPo

Two Roads, Etc. Dorothy Walters. IHMS

Two Rural Sisters. Charles Cotton. *Fr.* Resolution in Four Sonnets, of a Poetical Question, Concerning Four Rural Sisters. BoLoP

Two sculptors. Four Translations from the English of Robert Hershon. Robert Hershon. NeAC

Two Sec. Mods. Zulfikar Ghose. LP

Two Selves, The. Margaret Avison. NoAM

Two separate divided silences. Severed Selves. Dante Gabriel Rossetti. The House of Life, XL BoLoP; VPC

Two Sisters, The. *Unknown.* AIW; AmFP; MAT
    (Binnorie.) AIW

Two Songs. C. Day Lewis. NoAM

Two Songs. Adrienne Rich. NOBA; Psy

Two Songs from a Play. W. B. Yeats. *Fr.* The Resurrection. NOBE; OBP; PPoe; PPP

Two Sonnets. John Ashbery.
    Dido. CAPP; VGW
    Idiot, The. VGW

Two Spirits, The: an Allegory. Shelley. MBPR; Prf

Two Summers in Moravia. Roger McDonald. CAAP

Two Takes from Love in Los Angeles. Al Young. CoPAm

Two that could not have lived their single lives. Two in August. John Crowe Ransom. PPP

2001: The Tennyson/Hardy Poem. Gavin Ewart. FaBoCo

Two Tramps in Mud Time. Robert Frost. NoAM

Two Travellers, The. C. J. Boland. PFIr

Two Variations. Denise Levertov. PPoe
    Enquiry, *sel.* RiTi

Two Views of a Cadaver Room. Sylvia Plath. AnMo

Two Views of Two Ghost Towns. Charles Tomlinson. NoAM

Two voices are there: one is of the deep. A Sonnet. James Kenneth Stephen. FaBoCo; PPoD; SpRo

Two voices are there; one is of the sea. Thought of a Briton on the Subjugation of Switzerland. Wordsworth. MBPR; PBMP; SpRo

Two Voices in a Meadow. Richard Wilbur. PBMP

Two wedded hearts, if ere were such. Samuel Taylor Coleridge. MBPR

Two White Horses in a Line. *Unknown.* BluL

Two wild duck of the upland spaces. Duck. John Lyle Donaghy. BIrV

Two Witches, *sel.* Robert Frost.
    Witch of Coös, The. NoAM; NOBA; PAIC

Two Women. Naomi Replansky. NMM

Two Wrestlers. Robert Francis. SPo

'Twould ring the bells of Heaven. The Bells of Heaven. Ralph Hodgson. NOBE; PPoD

Tyger, The. Blake. See Tiger, The.

Tyger! Tyger! James Nolan. AATT

Tyger! Tyger! burning bright. *See* Tiger! Tiger! burning bright.

Tyndarus attempting too kis a fayre lasse with a long nose. Of Tyndarus, That Frumped a Gentlewoman. *Unknown, tr. by* Richard Stanyhurst. BIrV

Type of the antique Rome! Rich reliquary. The Coliseum. Poe. NOBA

Tyson's Corner. Primus St. John. PoBA

Tywater. Richard Wilbur. ConAP

U

U bet u wer. To a Poet I Knew. Jewel C. Latimore. PoBA

U feel that way sometimes. Mixed Sketches. Don L. Lee. BPo.

U Name This One. Carolyn M. Rodgers. NMM; PoBA

U. S. A., The. Grantland Rice. SPo

U.S. Coast and Geodetic Survey Ship *Pioneer*, The. Robert Hershon. NeAC

Ubi Iam Sunt? Richard L. Greene. PAIC

Ubi Sunt Qui ante Nos Fuerunt? *Unknown.* PAIC
    (Ubi Sunt? *longer version.*) OxBM

Ugly Child, The. Elizabeth Jennings. RAE

Ugly old man, An. No Great Matter. David Lawson. VGW

Ulalume—a Ballad. Poe. NOBA; PiAm

Ulivfak's Song of the Caribou. *Unknown, tr. fr. Caribou Eskimo.* AKE

Ultima Ratio Regum. Stephen Spender. LP; MPo; SFF

Ultima Thule. Longfellow. AmVN

Ultimate Anthology. Martin Bell. POL

Ultimate Antientropy, The. Theodore Weiss. NoAM

Ultimate Reality. Ogden Nash. FaBoCo

Ulysses. Dante, *tr. fr. Italian by* Longfellow. *Fr.* Divina Commedia: Inferno Epi

Ulysses. Robert Graves. NoAM

Ulysses. Tennyson. AnMo; Epi; HelP; InPK; InPS; IPWM; NOBE; PAIC; PPoe; PPP; SoSe

Ulysses and the Siren. Samuel Daniel. NOBE; PAIC

Ubaji Park. David Kherdian. SA

Umbilical. Eve Merriam. CTBA

Umh——uhumh! Umh——uhumh/Get a breath of that country air. Country Air. Mike Love *and* Brian Wilson. PoRo

Ummmmh oh ain't got no mama now. That Black Snake Moan. *Unknown.* BluL

Unaccustomed ripeness in the wood, An. Elizabeth. Robert Lowell. *Fr.* Harriet. CAPP; LoAs

Un-American Investigators. Langston Hughes. BPo

Unarm! unarm! No more your fights. Sir William Davenant. *Fr.* The Triumphs of the Prince D'Amour. SCP-2

Unbeliever, The. Elizabeth Bishop. NoAM

Unbounded is thy range; with varied style. The Stormy Hebrides. William Collins. *Fr.* An Ode on the Popular Superstitions. NOBE

Uncertainty. Wordsworth. *Fr.* Ecclesiastical Sonnets. MBPR

Uncessant minutes, whilst you move you tell. To His Watch When He Could Not Sleep. Lord Herbert of Cherbury. NOBE

Uncle Bull-boy. June Jordan. PoBA

Uncle Death. Walter Clark. NCSH

Uncle Dog: the Poet at 9. Robert Sward. VGW

Uncle Roderick. Norman MacCaig. MPo

Uncle sent for O. T. told him we have to fight. O. T.'s Blues. Waring Cuney. MAT

Unclench Yourself. Marge Piercy. NeAC

Uncomly in cloistre I cowre ful of care. Choristers Training. *Unknown.* OxBM

Unconsumable material is everywhere. The Square at Dawn. James Tate. NoAM

Undead, The. Richard Wilbur. CAPP; ConAP

Undefined Tenderness, An. Joel Oppenheimer. VGW

Under. George Bowering. NeAC

Under a lawn, than skies more clear. Upon Roses. Robert Herrick. SCP-1

Under a splintered mast. A Talisman. Marianne Moore. NCSH

Under a spreading chestnut-tree. The Village Blacksmith. Longfellow. AmVN

Under a swaying. El Dorado. Richard Ryan. BIrV

Under Ben Bulben. W. B. Yeats. NoAM; OxBTC

Under cracking pieces of the moon, eelpout. Spawning in Northern Minnesota. David McElroy. AmPA

Under great yellow flags and banners of the ancient cold. The Shadow of Cain. Edith Sitwell. OxBTC

KEY TO SYMBOLS

OFD	O Frabjous Day!: Poetry for Holidays and Special Occasions. *Myra Cohn Livingston, ed.* (1977) Atheneum
OLR	One Little Room, an Everywhere: Poems of Love. *Myra Cohn Livingston, ed.* (1975) Atheneum
OxBChV	Oxford Book of Children's Verse, The. *Iona and Peter Opie, eds.* (1973) Oxford University Press
OxBM	Oxford Book of Medieval English Verse, The. *Celia and Kenneth Sisam, eds.* (1970) Oxford University Press
OxBTC	*Oxford Book of Twentieth-Century English Verse, The. *Philip Larkin, ed.* (1973) Oxford University Press
PAIC	*Poetry and Its Conventions: An Anthology Examining Poetic Forms and Themes. *John T. Shawcross and Frederick R. Lapides, eds.* (1972) The Free Press
PBMP	*Premier Book of Major Poets, The: An Anthology. *Anita Dore, ed.* (1970) Fawcett Publications
PCat	Poetry of Cats, The. *Samuel Carr, ed.* (1974) The Viking Press
PeBB	*Penguin Book of Ballads, The. *Geoffrey Grigson, ed.* (1975) Penguin Books
PFD	Poems of Faith and Doubt: The Victorian Age. *R. L. Brett, ed.* (1970) University of South Carolina Press (First published in Great Britain, 1965, by Edward Arnold Publishers)
PFIr	Poems from Ireland. *William Cole, comp.* (1972) Thomas Y. Crowell Company
PiAm	Poet in America, The: 1650 to the Present. *Albert Gelpi, ed.* (1973) D. C. Heath and Company
PoBA	**Poetry of Black America, The: Anthology of the 20th Century. *Arnold Adoff, ed.* (1973) Harper & Row
POL	Poems One Line and Longer. *William Cole, ed.* (1973) Grossman Publishers
PoRo	Pop/Rock Songs of the Earth. *Jerry L. Walker, ed.* (1972) Scholastic Book Services (division of Scholastic Magazines, Inc.)
PoTa	Poet's Tales. The: A New Book of Story Poems. *William Cole, ed.* (1971) World Publishing
PPoD	Poetry: Points of Departure. *Henry Taylor, ed.* (1974) Winthrop Publishers
PPoe	*Pleasures of Poetry, The. *Donald Hall, ed.* (1971) Harper & Row
PPP	Poetry: Past and Present. *Frank Brady and Martin Price, eds.* (1974) Harcourt Brace Jovanovich
Prf	**Preferences: 51 American Poets Choose Poems from Their Own Work and from the Past. *Richard Howard, ed.* (1974) The Viking Press
PSN	Poems Since 1900: An Anthology of British and American Verse in the Twentieth Century. *Colin Falck and Ian Hamilton, eds.* (1975) Macdonald and Jane's (U. S. distributor: Beekman Publishers)

XV

Familiar Quotations

A collection of passages, phrases and proverbs traced to their sources in ancient and modern literature

FIFTEENTH AND 125TH ANNIVERSARY EDITION
REVISED AND ENLARGED

John Bartlett

Edited by EMILY MORISON BECK
and the editorial staff of Little, Brown and Company

LITTLE, BROWN AND COMPANY • BOSTON • TORONTO

Index of Authors

"It was the best of times,
It was the worst of times."

Though written in the Victorian Age, but not about the Victorian Age, this Dickens' line often applies to the way students feel about reading *Great Expectations*. The novel is difficult. It is one of Dickens' most critically acclaimed novels. *Great Expectations* contains great symbols, metaphors, and images, but it also contains great humor and humanity. In short, reading *Great Expectations* can be "the best of times," if we approach it with an open mind and try to understand how the Victorian Age affects the novel and how the novel can affect us, the modern reader.

"Wonderful party, wonderful games,
Wonderful unanimity, won-der-ful happiness!"

The question now is how do we approach this with an open mind and understand how the Victorian Age affects the novel and how the novel affects us, yet make this unit palatable? The answer lies in the term "Dickensian," which connotes a festive, convivial occasion, as the above quote from *A Christmas Carol* would indicate.

Through the use of a specific research project, we are going to have a theme party based on the Victorian Age and the works of Charles Dickens. During the month of December (there could not be a more appropriate time), we will be working on projects outlined below that will culminate in a "wonderful party" with "wonderful games" and "wonderful unanimity" and "wonderful happiness." That is our objective: that the reading of *Great Expectations* and studying the Victorian Age will lead to a Charles Dickens Festival!

"Facts alone are wanted in life."

Unlike the quote from *Hard Times,* facts are not quite alone in what we want, at least not in this project. There will not be a final test—unless you choose it. Instead, the festival will take the place of an exam; that is the true meaning of "Dickensian," replacing hardship with a party.

"A small matter to make these silly folks
so full of happiness."

As Scrooge found out, it is and it isn't such a small matter; you'll find this out, too, as you start the project. You will find instructions below for the two parts of the assignment.

Each student will be responsible for accomplishing:

1. A timeline of the Victorian Age
2. A project for the festival

Anyone not completing the assignments nor working effectively on the research will take a unit test on *Great Expectations*. Those are the facts.

Now consult the following sheets for instructions about the timeline and for ideas for your projects.

"Heaped up on the floor, to form a kind of throne,
were turkeys, geese, game, poultry, brawn. . .
barrels of oysters, red-hot chestnuts. . ."

Your grade and our festival could be even better than the Ghost of Christmas Present's "throne" if we operate with an open mind and work seriously. You need to consider what you want to do and how much "wonderful happiness" you want to create!

"It is a far, far better thing that I do. . ."

4–15   **VICTORIAN AGE TIMELINE**

1700 _____ **1800** _____ **1900**

On your own paper, draw a timeline based on the above dates. Fill in the following information on the timeline. This will work best if you use the paper lengthwise. There are many books in the media center with good examples of timelines, including:

Call Number   **Title**

_____   _____

_____   _____

_____   _____

1. Time period for the Victorian Age
2. Birthdate and date of death for Charles Dickens
3. Birth, coronation, and death dates for Queen Victoria
4. Date of the first World's Fair (The Crystal Palace)
5. Date of the first Reform Bill
6. Birth and death dates of Thomas Malthus
7. Date of the *Communist Manifesto*
8. Date of the first blast furnace
9. Date of the first steam railway
10. Date of the first steamship trans-Atlantic voyage
11. Date of the first telegraph
12. Date of the first trans-Atlantic cable
13. Birth and death dates for William Makepeace Thackeray
14. Dates of the Crimean War
15. Dates of the American Civil War
16. Dates of the American War of Independence
17. Birth and death dates for Jane Austen
18. Date *Origin of the Species* was published
19. Dates of Dickens' two trips to the United States
20. Approximate dates of the Industrial Revolution
21. Birth and death dates of Richard Wagner
22. Birth and death dates of Guiseppe Verdi

Name _____   Class _____

Date _____

1. Present a Victorian dance or song.

2. Report on Victorian fashion, dress, makeup, and hairstyles.

3. Report on Victorian manners.

4. Report on Victorian games and demonstrate them.

5. Present Victorian food and drink.

6. Report on Victorian decoration or architecture and give examples.

7. Report on Victorian holidays.

8. Dramatize an important scene in *Great Expectations* or in another Dickens' work.

9. Work on art for the Dickens Festival.

10. Prepare the menu and program for the Dickens Festival.

11. Your own choice to be confirmed with the teacher:

   _____

Your project will be:

_____

DECEMBER BULLETIN BOARDS

Winter Solstice
Pan American Health Day
Pearl Harbor Day
Human Rights Day
Nobel Prize Presentation Day
Bill of Rights Day
International Arbor Day
Hanukkah
Christmas
Canadian Boxing Day
John Lennon Remembrance Day
Forefathers' Day
Watch Night
New Year's Eve

Holiday Feasting

The December holidays are a time for celebrating around the world with special foods. A bulletin board illustrating holiday recipes can be attractive and informative as well.

You will need to select recipes from the many that are available in international cookbooks, books about holidays, and seasonal issues of your periodicals. If you want to be able to include pictures of the dishes, your selection may be guided by the availability of those pictures in withdrawn magazines or newspapers. The *New York Times* and the *Christian Science Monitor* are excellent sources of holiday menus and recipes with an ethnic or international flavor. Perhaps the homemaking teacher has illustrations to lend.

The material you will need are:

- Red wrapping paper for the background

- Green foil wrapping paper

- An 8- to 10-foot garland of artificial greens or tinsel

- Bright white letter-size paper, one for each recipe

- Rubber cement

- Stapler

To make the bulletin board:

1. Cover the bulletin board with red wrapping paper. Swag a rope of artificial greens across the top of the board. You can also make a garland of foil by cutting 2″ × 10″ strips of green foil. You will need enough strips to form an 8- to 10-foot chain. Use the paper cutter to make these strips quickly; they need not be absolutely uniform. Cement the strips into circles, interlocking them one with another as you work. If the foil is two colors, front and back, alternate the sides that are exposed.

2. Cut letters two to three inches high from green foil to spell out your caption of "Holiday Feasting." Center the caption at the top of the board.

3. Prepare "posters" of recipes and pictures on the white paper. Print with felt-tip pen, type, or prepare the recipes on a computer. The Fontrix℠ program for the IBM/PC allows selection of print type and size, and also the addition of graphics that could take the place of other illustrations.

4. Each recipe should be identified with its name and the country of origin. Staple these sheets to the bulletin board. Decorate each recipe with a green foil pinwheel. The pinwheels and the garland add dimension to your display. To make the pinwheels:

- Cut 6-inch squares from the green foil, one for each recipe.
- Cut in from each corner diagonally to about one inch from the center.
- Bring every other point in to the center of the square, overlapping them.
- Staple through the points into the board.

INSERVICE AND PUBLIC RELATIONS: GIFT SUGGESTIONS AND MEDIA CENTER FESTIVITIES

December is a gift exchange month for very nearly everyone. You can provide a service to teachers and students by offering suggestions for gifts and sources for obtaining them.

In your mail you usually receive mail order gift catalogs as well as holiday catalogs from book distributors. After you have stamped these catalogs with your property stamp, attach a reserve card to each one with a paper clip and suggest that staff and students borrow them for overnight. Collect them in magazine files and display them at the circulatoin desk or on the card catalog.

The *New York Times Book Review* section of the Sunday *New York Times* will have a Christmas gift issue. You will find holiday gift sections in other periodicals as well. As these arrive, prepare them as you do the catalogs for overnight circulation. Include among these items your current catalogs and flyers about video and computer programs since videocassette recorders and computers are now popular equipment in homes.

Copy the bestseller lists from the *New York Times* and your regional and local newspapers. Post these lists on your informational bulletin board under an identifying caption, such as "Great Gifts" or "Gifts That Last."

The ALA publishes attractive bibliographies of outstanding and notable books on many topics and for diverse groups such as the college-bound or reluctant readers. These also make excellent suggestions for gifts and could be posted with the bestsellers.

Here are three quotations you might consider posting with your lists of books:

" *'Tis the good reader that makes the good book.*"
Ralph Waldo Emerson
Success

"There is an art of reading, as well as an art of thinking, and an art of writing."
Isaac D'Israeli
Literary Character

"Reading is to the mind what exercise is to the body."
Joseph Addison
The Tatler

With everyone eagerly awaiting the holiday break, it is difficult for students to stay on task or for you to feel that you are being very productive. Pope John's advice in *Journal of the Soul* is pertinent at this time:

*"See everything
Overlook a lot
Correct a little"*

Remembering that December should be a joyous season, you may plan some festive activities for the media center. A few suggestions are:

1. Ask a music instructor to prepare a short program of madrigals, carols, or other holiday music with a vocal group or a small instrumental ensemble. Invite them to perform in the media center during lunch periods.

2. Invite one of the art teachers, or a person from the community, to demonstrate gift-wrapping with unusual materials at a 20-minute workshop for students and teachers. This can take place in the media center during an activity period or immediately after school. To make this as easy as possible for the presenter, offer to collect the materials and tools and to make all arrangements.

3. Rent a videotape or film appropriate for the season, and arrange for continuous showings in an area of the media center, in the cafeteria or lounge, or in an available classroom.

January

"This day Time winds the exhausted chain,
To run the twelvemonth's length again . . .'

Robert Burns
Sketch—New Year's Day

January Birthdays

106 B.C.	Cicero
1561	Francis Bacon
1622	Molière
1706	Benjamin Franklin
1737	Thomas Paine
1759	Robert Burns
1809	Edgar Allan Poe
1832	Lewis Carroll
1862	Edith Wharton
1876	Jack London
1878	Carl Sandburg
1882	Virginia Woolf
1892	J.R.R. Tolkien
1896	John Dos Passos
1905	Eric Frank Russell
1905	John O'Hara
1919	Vera Cleaver
1919	J.D. Salinger
1925	Robert Cormier
1928	William Kennedy
1932	Umberto Eco
1935	Robert Silverberg
1937	Joseph Wambaugh

MANAGEMENT TASKS

---

*"What's amiss I'll strive to mend,
and endure what can't be mended."*

Isaac Watts
Good Resolutions

The management tasks for the month of January are:

1. Managing administrative records
2. Building a vertical file collection

Managing Administrative Records

Records management is an integral part of the administrative duties of school media specialists. It is imperative that we gain control of the information that is necessary for an effective, efficient management program. We are, in many respects, operating the offices of small businesses.

For many of us, this is a difficult aspect of our jobs, and, consequently, an area we often neglect. Our training and exposure to the concepts of records management may be minimal; time to devote to the process is always a restrictive factor; the absence of qualified clerical personnel is invariably an obstacle.

A few of the factors that have contributed to the undesirable status of records control in school media center offices are:

- Duplication of records with the advent of copying machines
- Application of computer technology to library management tasks
- Integration of library and audiovisual services into one administrative unit
- Increase in support staffing with more persons involved, or the decrease with too few people involved
- Increased scope of responsibilities assigned to personnel in the media center

Conditions that show readily the need for efficient records management are often apparent in our offices:

- Scarcity of funds for office equipment
- Low priority assigned to equipment purchases for data management in the media center
- Lack of space for new technology
- Proliferation of records and the diversity of format
- Unsatisfactory retrieval time
- Ambiguous filing responsibilities
- Outdated filing systems
- Lack of continuity in personnel assignments

90

The process for developing a records management system starts with an evaluation of the current status of the records in your files, proceeds through the development of standards and guidelines for the retention and disposal of records, and is completed with the assistance you provide for support personnel to whom you assign the management tasks.

The strategies you can employ to complete this process are as follows:

Step 1. Survey the records presently in your files. Determine their nature and format, and classify them as legal, administrative, or historical. Few of your records will fall into the legal category since most will be duplicates of files in the central business office.

Step 2. Decide what records you may be producing which would fall under state or local regulations. A call to the district business administrator may be necessary to determine this. For example, if you hold the warranties on equipment, the service contracts, or the inventory records of equipment, there are state regulations about the retention of these.

Step 3. Develop a form for a thorough inventory of your records. I have provided one for your use.

Step 4. Construct a time table for completing the records inventory.

Step 5. Assign the inventory task. The person who is most familiar with the records, who references them most often, is the logical person to receive this assignment.

Step 6. Using the inventory as your source of information, with particular concern for the frequency of reference to the files, prepare a schedule for retention and disposal of the records. A sample form for this purpose is included in the Appendix.

Thoreau's advice in *Walden* certainly applies to records management in the school media center office: "Simplify, simplify, simplify." Discourage the generating of five copies of a funds transfer request if one will do; do not retain ten years' worth of purchase orders if you refer only to those of the past two; centralize your budget accounts, even though purchase orders may be produced at more than one work station.

The completion of this process for development of a records management program will give you important information for the decisions you will make next month regarding automating media center procedures.

Building a Vertical File Collection

Once you provide subject access to a vertical file of topics, you will discover students will pass up other sources in favor of this data. The selection of material has been made for them; generally, the information is concise; and the illustrated material can prove to be the kind unavailable elsewhere.

Since the vertical file may be such a popular resource in your media center, you need to plan for its development and maintenance.

First, what subjects should you choose to include?

1. Tune in to the reference questions students are asking; review regularly the log you have established for this purpose.
2. Listen to and read the daily bulletin to learn what topics clubs are discussing and what activities are popular.
3. Familiarize yourself with the curriculum guides you obtained in the fall.
4. Ask the department chairpersons to suggest current topics.

5. Look for lesson plans every chance you get, even those that do not involve media center research directly.

6. Include subjects teachers will have personal interests in, such as travel items, tax information, graduate programs or study opportunities

Selecting materials about the topics for your vertical file is an ongoing task. There are many sources you may consider for appropriate items:

1. Some items will be discoveries among the materials that cross your desk.

2. The *Vertical File Index* from H.W. Wilson

3. Catalogs of free or inexpensive materials

4. *Public Affairs* pamphlets

5. Requests from specific agencies, groups, or individuals

6. Clippings from discarded materials

Collect items for the vertical file in one designated spot. Though you may come across materials daily, assigning the subject headings and preparing the items for the file, as well as the filing, are tasks that require a block of time.

Preparing materials for the file involves the following steps:

1. Clearly indicate the source and date of each item on the item itself.

2. Stamp each item with your property stamp.

3. Print "V.F." and the assigned subject heading on the item.

4. If the heading you assign is new to the file, print that heading on a manila file folder and add the item to it.

5. Establish the subject heading in a vertical file shelf list.

6. Instruct the typist to type two subject cards that indicate "**See Vertical File.**"

7. File one card in the shelf list and one in the public catalog.

8. Prepare cross-reference headings for vertical file materials just as you do for other materials in the catalog.

LIBRARY RESEARCH PLAN

Level I: *Kaleidoscope*

The objectives for this library research plan are as follows:

• The students will learn the location of the reference tool called *Kaleidoscope*. (NOTE: It was formerly called *Deadline Data*.)

• The students will learn the kind of information to be found in this resource.

• The students will complete a skills exercise to demonstrate their ability to locate information in *Kaleidoscope*.

• The students will apply this skill to a research task assigned in social studies.

Make copies of Figures 5-1 through 5-8 for your students. Here is the answer key for the skills exercise:

1. Yes
2. Update
3. 776 B.C.
4. 9,010
5. Association of Southeast Asian Nations

6. Pula
7. Summaries will vary
8. County
9. 1960
10. Summaries will vary

Level II: American History

The objectives for this library research plan are as follows:

- The students will select important persons from American history and research their lives.
- The students will read and draw conclusions about those persons' influence upon the course of history.
- The students will communicate their ideas in written form, including bibliographic references.
- The students will gain experience in the use of general, historical biographical references.
- The students will use non-print secondary sources.
- The students will experience the use of biography to understand history.

You'll need copies of Figures 5–9 and 5–10 for your students.

Level III: Business Education

The objectives for this library research plan are as follows:

- The students will locate current information about computer applications by using subject entries in periodical indexes.
- The students will use headings and subheadings to narrow a topic.
- The students will use the card catalog to locate computer programs and other non-print sources of information.
- The students will take notes, cite their references accurately, and write a two-page research paper about their topic.

Make copies of Figures 5–11 through 5–13, and distribute them to your students.

Name _____   Class _____

Date _____

GUIDE FOR *KALEIDOSCOPE*

    Kaleidoscope is a file of current world data. The information is printed on 5″ × 8″ cards and is updated regularly. These files of cards are arranged alphabetically by country.

    Each country file includes statistical information, data about the government, a chronology of news events, and historical background about the country.

    In addition to the country files, there are sections in *Kaleidoscope* for:

- International organizations
- Metric system
- Obituaries
- Sports
- World currency rates
- World population table
- Weekly news summary
- Bibliography

    The United States and Canada files are expanded to include information about individual states and provinces.

    In the media center, *Kaleidoscope* is located _____

_____ .

Name _____   Class _____

Date _____

KALEIDOSCOPE SKILLS EXERCISE   5–2

Look at the illustrations of *Kaleidoscope* file cards. Now find the answers to the following questions in your media center's *Kaleidoscope* files.

1. Does the state of Texas allow the death penalty?

   _____

2. What is the per capita income in the state of New Hampshire?

   _____

3. Where were the winter Olympic games held?

   _____

4. How many miles of coast line are in China?

   _____

5. What is the full name for the acronym ASEAN?

   _____

   _____

6. What is the name for the unit of currency in Botswana?

   _____

7. Summarize one event that occurred in the past six months that was reported in the ''Weekly News'' section.

   _____

   _____

8. What is the name of the Milwaukee Brewers' home stadium?

   _____

9. In what year did Great Britain inaugurate a ten-year changeover to the metric system?

   _____

10. On the back of this sheet, summarize one important event that occurred in Spain in 1986.

(PAGE 1)

Kaleidoscope:
CURRENT WORLD DATA
© 1987 by ABC-CLIO, Inc.
Santa Barbara, CA 93140-4397

ABC-CLIO

[continued on reverse side]

CHINA
GENERAL DATA AND GOVERNMENT

(see also: Chronology, History)

LOCATION: Covering a major part of eastern Asia, China is bordered by Mongolia to the north, the Soviet Union to the north and west, Afghanistan and Pakistan to the west, and India, Nepal, Bhutan, Burma, Laos and Vietnam to the south. North Korea also borders China at a north-eastern section, while China's coastline is formed along the Pacific Ocean.

AREA: 3,695,500 sq. miles

Land Use: 74.30% desert, waste, or urban; 11.00% cropland; 12.70% forest and woodland; 2.00% inland water.

Arable Land: 11%

Arable Land per capita: 0.25 acres

Coastline: 9,010 miles

Land Borders: 14,914 miles

CAPITAL: Beijing (Peking)

TIME:
   15 hours earlier than US Eastern Standard

[Issued Jan 26, 1986]

ASEAN
Association of South East Asian Nations
GENERAL DATA

see also: CHRONOLOGY sections for member nations

The Association of South East Asian Nations (ASEAN) was formally established at Bangkok, Thailand on Aug 9, 1967. ASEAN's stated purpose is "to accelerate economic growth, social progress and cultural development" among member nations, as well as to "promote active collaboration and mutual assistance...in the economic, social, cultural, technical, scientific and administrative fields." It is not a military alliance.

MEMBERSHIP
Indonesia (headquarters), Brunei, Malaysia, Philippines, Singapore and Thailand. *Observer status*: Papua New Guinea.

ORGANIZATION
The Summit Meeting is the highest authority of the organization, and includes the government heads from each member nation.

[Issued Sep 19, 1988]

Kaleidoscope:
CURRENT WORLD DATA
© 1988 by ABC-CLIO, Inc.
Santa Barbara, CA 93140-4397

ABC-CLIO

(PAGE 1)

Ministerial Meetings of foreign ministers from the member states convene annually. They are responsible for the adoption of the group's policies. Economic and other ministers from the member countries meet as needed.

The Standing Committee meets for consultations, as necessary, between ministerial meetings. It is composed of the foreign minister of the host country, ambassadors from the remaining member nations and certain ASEAN officials.

A permanent **Secretariat**, formed in 1976, is the central coordinating body. Every three years the post of Secretary-General rotates alphabetically (by country name) among member nations.

Secretary-General: Roderick Yong Yin Fatt (Brunei).

There are 5 economic **Committees** (Food, Agriculture & Forestry; Transportation & Communications; Trade &

[continued on reverse side]

Reverse side of WORLD CURRENCY RATES   (PAGE 2)

COUNTRY	CURRENCY UNIT	UNIT PER US$ JUL 4, 1988	UNIT PER US$ MAR 23, 1988
Bolivia	Boliviano	2.41	2.25
Botswana	Pula	1.88	1.71
Brazil	Cruzado	196.49	110.79
Britain	Pound	0.59	0.54
Brunei	Dollar	2.07	2.02
Bulgaria	Lev	0.86	0.83
Burkina Faso	CFA Franc	308.16	287.55
Burma	Kyat	6.87	6.22
Burundi	Franc	150.42	117.68
Cambodia	Riel	101.13	100.00

METRIC SYSTEMS/MEASURES

HISTORY OF METRIC SYSTEM, cont'd

(PAGE 3)

Kaleidoscope:
CURRENT WORLD DATA
© 1988 by ABC-CLIO, Inc.
Santa Barbara, CA 93140-4397

1795 . . . .   France officially adopts the metric system but permits the people to utilize other measurement units until 1840.

1821 . . . .   US Secretary of State John Quincy Adams proposes conversion to the metric system; however, Congress rejects the idea.

1837 . . . .   French Government passes a law requiring all Frenchmen to begin to use the metric system as of Jan 1, 1840.

1866 . . . .   US Congress legalizes the metric system but does not require its use.

1870-75 . . . .   International metric convention creates new measurement standards for the base units of length and mass.

1875 . . . .   Seventeen nations participating in the international metric convention sign the Treaty of the Meter, which provides for the International Bureau of Weights and Measures, a permanent organization to change the metric system as necessary.

1893 . . . .   US bases the yard and the pound on fractions of the standard meter and kilogram.

1900 . . . .   By the turn of the century, 35 nations have adopted the metric system.

1957 . . . .   US Army and Marine Corps adopt the metric system for their weapons and equipment.

1960 . . . .   General Conference of Weights and Measures, attended by the countries using the metric system, adopts the current version of the system.

1965 . . . .   Britain inaugurates a 10-year changeover to the metric system.

1968-71 . . . .   US congressional study examines the problems involved in metric conversion and recommends that the US implement a 10-year step-by-step conversion to the metric system.

1970 . . . .   Canada and Australia create a commission to plan conversion to the metric measurement system.

Issued Sep 26, 1988

[continued on reverse side]

Kaleidoscope:
CURRENT WORLD DATA
© 1988 by ABC-CLIO, Inc.
Santa Barbara, CA 93140-4397

ABC-CLIO

(PAGE 1)

SPORTS-OLYMPICS

OLYMPIC GAMES:
HISTORY & ORGANIZATION

ANCIENT OLYMPICS

Dates: The first recorded Olympiad took place in 776 B.C. The ancient games continued at 4-year intervals until they were banned in 394 A.D.

Site: Olympia (southwestern Greece)

Events: Foot races, chariot races, discus throw, boxing, wrestling

MODERN OLYMPICS

Dates: The first modern Olympiad was held in 1896. The modern summer games have continued at 4-year intervals since then except for 1916, 1940 and 1944. Starting in 1924, there have been parallel winter games.

Site: The modern Olympics move from site to site (see lists on following pages).

Events: There were 46 events at the 1988 Winter Olympics in the following sports: Alpine skiing, Nordic skiing and jumping, biathlon, ice hockey, bobsled, luge, figure skating and speed skating. In the 1984 Summer Olympics there were 220 separate competitive events in the following sports: archery, basketball, boxing, canoeing, cycling, fencing, field hockey, gymnastics, handball, horsemanship, judo, modern pentathlon, rowing, shooting, soccer, water polo, swimming and diving, track and field, volleyball, weight-lifting, wrestling and yachting.

[continued on reverse side]

[Issued Sep 5, 1988]

Kaleidoscope:
CURRENT WORLD DATA
© 1986 by ABC-Clio, Inc.
ABC-CLIO Santa Barbara, CA 93140-4397

T E X A S   (page 86)

STATE FINANCES: Taxes (per capita): $614.75 (1984)
Income (per capita): $11,685 (1983)
Sales & gross receipts taxes (%): 4% (since 1971)
Personal income tax: no
Lottery: no

Educational expenditures per pupil: $2,913 (1984)

Business or tax information
Comptroller
Public Accounts
LBJ Bldg. Rm. 104
Austin, TX 78774
(512) 475-1900

State tourist office
Tourist Development Agency
Capitol Station
P.O. Box 12008
Austin, TX 78711
(512) 475-4326

Legal drinking age: 19

Minimum age for driving license
                (unrestricted): 16

Nuclear energy: Four nuclear plans have construction permits (1984)

Death Penalty: yes, last execution was in 1986

[continued on next page] [Issued Jul 21, 1986]

Name _____   Class _____

Date _____

5–9   **AMERICAN HISTORY ASSIGNMENT**

"All history is biography."
Samuel Johnson

Was Samuel Johnson right? Do individuals shape and change the events we call "history"?

Select a person you believe made an important contribution to American life. This person may be a statesman, an explorer, a philosopher, a scientist, an educator, an artist—anyone from any walk of life.

Using resources in your media center, learn about your chosen individual's life. Write an essay that will:

- Summarize the person's contribution to our history

- Tell about the period in which the person lived

- Include information about the person's individual development

- Tell why you consider this person important

Whatever the person's career or life's work, your task is to support your belief that he or she made history. Your essay should be _____ in length. Include a bibliography of sources, and foot-note any quotes.

Due date is _____.

Name _____   Class _____

Date _____

GUIDE TO AMERICAN HISTORY   5–10

     To complete your assignment in American history, you will use biographical reference materials as well as autobiographies (921), collected biographies (920), and individual biographies (921).

     To get started, you may want to use general sources such as:

Call Number	Title
_____	*Dictionary of American Biography*
_____	*Webster's Biographical Dictionary*
_____	*Who's Who*
_____	*Who Was Who in America*
_____	_____

     Use the name of the person you have chosen as a subject entry to the card catalog and to periodical indexes.

     Do not neglect the material you will find in the media center in audiovisual format, in microfiche programs, and in the vertical files.

5–11   BUSINESS EDUCATION ASSIGNMENT

1. You are to research the application of computer technology to a particular field, such as computers in medicine.

2. Confirm your topic with your teacher.

   TOPIC: _____

   _____

3. Your media specialist will review the process of using specific resources for this assignment. This will include the use of subject headings and subheadings in the resources to narrow a topic. The sample illustrations will help you.

4. Take notes as you proceed with your research, remembering to include the bibliographic information necessary for citing the sources you have found to be useful. This saves time and the necessity for retracing your steps. If you wish to quote a particular source, give credit where credit is due!

5. Your paper should include *three* sources of information, one of which must be a periodical article written within the past six months. This may be a newspaper article if it is no longer than one column in length. Since your topics are to be researched in current sources, you will use:

   Readers' Guide to Periodical Literature
   NewsBank®
   New York Times Current Events on Microfiche
   New York Times Index

   _____

   As you use these subject indexes, be aware of the subheadings, and the "see also," and "see" references. These entry words and phrases will help you to narrow your topic.

   The card catalog should be checked to see whether there are vertical files, computer programs, or other non-print programs available in the media center about your topic.

6. Your paper should be approximately two pages in length, written in your own words. Your

   paper is due on _____ .

54 READERS' GUIDE TO PERIODICAL LITERATURE

COMPUTER PROGRAMMING—See also—*cont.*
  Computers—Mathematical use—Programming
  Computers—Musical use—Programming
  Computers—Operating systems
  Computers—Physics use—Programming
  Computers—Printing use—Programming
  Computers—Religious use—Programming
  Computers—Sports use—Programming
  Computers—Tax return use—Programming
  Data structures (Computer science)
  Desktop publishing—Programming
  File organization (Computers)
  Spreadsheets (Computer programs)
  Word processors and processing—Programming
AmigaView. S. Leemon. See issues of Compute!
The beginner's page. C. Regena. See issues of Compute!
Cursor plus. E. Gendrano and G. Knauss. il *Compute!* 10:64-5 Mr '88
The elementary Amiga (IV) [special directories, logical devices, and timesaving command files] J. Butterfield. *Compute!* 10:69-70 Mr '88
IBM personal computing. D. B. Trivette. See issues of Compute!
Insight: Atari. B. Wilkinson. See issues of Compute!
ST outlook. P. I. Nelson. See issues of Compute!
COMPUTER SCIENCE *See* Computers
COMPUTER SECURITY *See* Computers—Security measures
COMPUTER SERVICE INDUSTRIES
  See also
  Advanced Software Inc.
  Ashton-Tate, Inc.
  Control Data Corp.
  Index Technology (Firm)
  International Business Machines Corp.
Marketing
A market is born out of computer confusion [systems integration business] C. Brown. il *Business Week* p124-5 Ap 25 '88
Japan
A new look in mainframes. S. Glazer. il *High Technology Business* 8:15 Ap '88
The wizard of TRON [K. Sakamura's The Real-time Operating system Nucleus] il *World Press Review* 35:58 Ap '88
United States
  See Computer service industries
COMPUTER SIMULATION
  See also
  Flight simulators
Simulating a mountain's shadow. B. E. Schaefer. il *Sky and Telescope* 75:416-18 Ap '88
COMPUTER SOFTWARE *See* Computer programming
COMPUTER SOFTWARE INDUSTRY *See* Computer service industries
COMPUTER STORAGE DEVICES *See* Computers—Memory systems
COMPUTER TERMINALS
  See also
  Information display systems
COMPUTER VIRUSES
The Amiga virus [with diagnostic program] J. Butterfield. il *Compute!* 10:48-9 Mr '88
The Trojan wars. A. R. Levitan. *Compute!* 10:59 Mr '88
COMPUTER WORKSTATIONS *See* Workstations
COMPUTER WORMS *See* Computer viruses
COMPUTERS
  See also
  Automation
  Hackers (Computer enthusiasts)
  Information storage and retrieval systems
  Neural network computers
  Reduced instruction set computers
  Supercomputers
AmigaView. S. Leemon. See issues of Compute!
Build the PT-68K (VI). P. Stark. il *Radio-Electronics* 59 ComputerDigest:98-100 Ap '88
Don't leave home without one [laptop computers] P. Elmer-Dewitt. il *Time* 131:87 Ap 18 '88
Microscope. S. Leemon. See issues of Compute!
The world inside the computer. F. D'Ignazio. See issues of Compute!
Access control
  See Computers—Security measures
Architectural use
  Programming
Software reviews for architects [Intergraph MicroStation Version 2.0 and Lotus Manuscript Release 1.0] S. S. Ross. il *Architectural Record* 176:125+ Ap '88

Art use
Creative computers. M. Rogers. il *Newsweek* 111:54-5 Ap 25 '88
  Programming
AutoCAD and AutoSketch, by Autodesk. il *Radio-Electronics* 59 ComputerDigest:88-90 Ap '88
Color pad [Commodore drawing program] F. Bentley. il *Compute!* 10:72-82 Mr '88
Postcards. E. Bobo. il *Compute!* 10:25-6 Mr '88
Astronomical use
Comet source: close to Neptune [Oort cloud; computer simulation of orbital dynamics by Martin Duncan and others] R. A. Kerr. *Science* 239:1372-3 Mr 18 '88
Automotive use
  See also
  Automobiles—Electronic equipment
Aviation use
  See also
  Inertial guidance systems
USAF will begin precision tests of C-130 nav/com system. K. J. Stein. il *Aviation Week & Space Technology* 128:87+ Ap 25 '88
Biological use
  Programming
DNA telephone game [computer analysis of bacterial genes; work of James A. Lake] R. Harris. *Oceans* 21:56 Mr/Ap '88
Succeeding technologies [L. Korn and C. Queen] E. Dyson. il *Forbes* 141 Ann Directory:122 Ap 25 '88
Business use
  See also
  Offices—Automation
  Telecommuting
Apple's corporate image: Macintosh's new popularity changes computing. A. M. Seybold. il *High Technology Business* 8:13 Ap '88
Streamlining the offices of today—from storage to work flow [special section] il *Working Woman* 13:55-8+ Ap '88
Circuits
  See Integrated circuits
Compatibility
Solving the IBM-compatibles puzzle [cover story] S. Morgenstern. il *Family & Home Office Computing* 6:41-7 Mr '88
Control use
Build REACTS: the Radio-Electronics Advanced Control System (III). H. E. Roberts. il *Radio-Electronics* 59:52-4 Ap '88
Design
Computers of the future. F. D'Ignazio. *Compute!* 10:58 Mr '88
Drugstore use
  See Drugstores—Automation
Educational use
Education and technology [address, October 28, 1987] J. H. Zumberge. *Vital Speeches of the Day* 64:367-9 Ap 1 '88
  Programming
Software to raise SAT scores. K. Kane. il *Family & Home Office Computing* 6:32+ Mr '88
Exhibitions
Centerstage: Amiga! The World of Commodore Show. N. Randall. il *Compute!* 10:44-6 Mr '88
Editor's notes [computers at the Winter Consumer Electronics Show] K. Ferrell and S. Bateman. *Compute!* 10:4 Mr '88
Export-import trade use
PCs on the high seas [computerizing export operations] S. Golob. il *Nation's Business* 76:28 Ap '88
Financial services use
  See also
  Computers—Tax return use
  Programming
Financial planning software can make money management less taxing. S. Miller. *Black Enterprise* 18:43 Ap '88
Gambling use
  Programming
Casino blackjack. J. Hamilton. il *Compute!* 10:30-1+ Mr '88
Geological use
Formation of the Rocky Mountains, western United States: a continuum computer model. P. Bird. bibl f il maps *Science* 239:1501-7 Mr 25 '88
Image processing use
  See Image processing
Industrial use
  See also
  Automation

AVIATION
   See **Air Travel**

AZT
   See **AIDS (Acquired Immune Deficiency Syndrome)** – treatment

BABY BOOM GENERATION
   See **Social Conditions and Trends** – baby boom generation

BABY FOOD
   See **Food** – baby food

BABYSITTING
   See **Child Care** – babysitting services

BAHAMAS
   drugs
      trafficking – 1988 INT 58:D6–7

BAKKER, JIM
   lawsuits and court orders
      return to PTL – 1988 SOC 53:D6
   publicity – 1988 SOC 53:B10

BALDNESS
   research
      causes – 1988 HEA 60:A7

BALLOTS
   See **Initiatives and Referenda**

BANGERTER, NORMAN H.
   gubernatorial primary candidacy, 1988 (Utah)
      campaign issues – 1988 POL 50:A8

BANK CREDIT CARDS
   See **Credit Cards** – bank cards

BANKRUPTCY
   [Bankruptcy in particular industries may be found under name of industry]
   See also **Finance, Personal** – bankruptcy, personal
   statistics
      charts – 1988 BUS 49:D8–9

BANKS AND BANKING
   See also **Credit; Credit Unions; Financial Services and Investments; Savings and Loan Associations**
   branch banking
      attitudes and opinions (chart)
         Montana – 1988 BUS 49:D10–11
   checking accounts
      increased fees (chart)
         Florida – 1988 CON 13:C6–8
   community banks
      industry conditions
         Indiana – 1988 BUS 49:D12–13
   competition
      . . .
      Vermont – 1988 BUS 49:D14–E1
   credit cards
      See **Credit Cards** – bank cards
   deposit insurance
      charts
         Texas – 1988 BUS 49:E2–4
   electronic banking
      at home services
         Georgia – 1988 CON 13:C9
      automatic teller machines
         Illinois – 1988 CON 13:C10
         Maine – 1988 CON 13:C11
         Ohio – 1988 CON 13:C12

BANKS AND BANKING (continued)
   financial problems
      studies and reports
         Alaska – 1988 BUS 49:E5–7
   foreign banks in U.S.
      Japanese (chart) – 1988 BUS 49:E8–9
   fraud and misuse of funds
      arrests and indictments – 1988 BUS 49:E10–11
   industry conditions
      charts – 1988 BUS 49:E12–13
         Florida – 1988 BUS 49:E14–F1
         Texas – 1988 BUS 49:F2–3
   interest rates
      See also **Mortgages** – interest rates
   interstate banking
      charts
         Minnesota – 1988 BUS 49:F4–6
      laws and legislation
         Minnesota – 1988 BUS 49:F7–8
         Pennsylvania – 1988 BUS 49:F9
   labor-management relations
      layoffs
         California – 1988 EMP 31:D9–10
   loans
      See also **Mortgages**
      disclosures
         Texas – 1988 CON 13:C13–14
      repayment scams
         international credit firms – 1988 INT 58:D8–10
   minority banks
      shortages
         Florida: Jacksonville – 1988 BUS 49:F10–11
   regulation
      laws and legislation – 1988 BUS 49:F12–13
      studies and reports – 1988 BUS 49:F14–G2
   savings accounts
      educational tool
         California – 1988 CON 13:D1–3
      increased fees (chart) – 1988 CON 13:C6–8
   services
      cashing government checks
         Ohio – 1988 CON 13:D4
   studies and reports
      charts
         California – 1988 CON 13:D5–6

BAPTIST CHURCH
   crusades, rallies, etc.
      singles weekend
         Tennessee: Nashville – 1988 SOC 51:E14
   divisions and mergers
      conservatives vs. moderates – 1988 SOC 52:A5
      fundamentalists vs. moderates – 1988 SOC 52:A6
   religious education
      seminaries, new president
         North Carolina: Southeastern Baptist Theological Seminary – 1988 SOC 52:G8, 52:G7
   religious literature
      hymnal revision – 1988 SOC 52:G10
   women ministers
      conservative opposition – 1988 SOC 53:F5–7

BAR ASSOCIATIONS
   See **Lawyers and Law Firms** – bar associations

BARS AND TAVERNS
   See also **Drunken Driving** – accidents, liability; **Legal Drinking Age**
   happy hours
      rulings
         Delaware – 1988 BUS 49:G3

JANUARY BULLETIN BOARDS

New Year's Day
Martin Luther King, Jr., Day
Emancipation Proclamation Anniversary
Sherlock Holmes' ''Birthday''
World Literacy Day
Stephen Foster Memorial
Vietnam Day
Baseball Hall of Fame Anniversary

I Resolve . . .

Your message for January will be self-improvement through resolutions to change undesirable habits or behavior patterns. Use the symbol used internationally to indicate ''not permitted'' (circle with a diagonal line through it).

You will need:

- A number of uniformly-sized pieces of brightly colored construction paper
- Letters for your caption
- Wide-tip markers

Find illustrations in discarded materials to attach to the ''not permitted'' signs, or use simple line drawings. Some suggestions are:

- a lit cigarette
- drugs
- alcohol
- junk foods

Following this theme, you might highlight books and other materials from your collection about self-improvement, understanding oneself and others, exercise, nutrition, developing proper study habits, dealing with family problems, and other topics of concern to adolescents.

INSERVICE AND PUBLIC RELATIONS:
PROMOTING USE OF NON-PRINT MATERIALS

Information is available in an ever-increasing variety of formats. As a media specialist, you have a mission: to acquire resources for students and teachers in both print and non-print formats that are effective in the learning process.

Even though you may rely upon recommendations from supervisors and teachers for curriculum-related materials, you may find use of those materials after purchase to be limited. You might question the validity of dedicating money from your budget to the purchase of audiovisuals.

There are several reasons your non-print collection may be under-utilized:

1. The materials may have been poorly selected.
2. Teachers and students may not be aware of the collection.
3. Teachers and students may be inexperienced in the use of audiovisuals.
4. Scheduling the use of equipment may be inconvenient, and it may be difficult to locate materials when needed.

For a number of reasons, you may decide that an audiovisual program was a poor selection. It may be of poor quality, may not be suitable for your school, or it may convey very biased, inaccurate or outdated information. Such a program is a candidate for withdrawal at the time of inventory, and it is subject to evaluation according to your established policies for weeding, just as the print materials in your collection are. By careful previewing of materials, you can hope to avoid purchasing questionable programs in the future.

Given the reticence on the part of some teachers, as well as students, to use audiovisual materials, you need to promote awareness of the materials. When preparing bibliographies for units or special interests, include the appropriate audiovisual titles; take new materials to department meetings for "show and tell," include new acquisitions as a regular feature in your newsletters to faculty, and request time at a faculty meeting to promote a new program.

You might ask that a faculty meeting be held in the media center. At that time, you could group materials by department and ask that teachers take time after the business meeting to browse. Have the necessary equipment available for previewing right then and there. When a new program is acquired, a copy of the guide should be made and routed to appropriate supervisors and teachers. Use every device possible to let your staff and students know what is available for their use.

Perhaps the most prevalent reason teachers and students do not use audiovisual materials is that they are uncomfortable doing so. So many things can go wrong! Several strategies for helping them gain experience with the process are:

1. Use non-print media at every opportunity when you are presenting skills lessons to classes or making presentations at meetings.
2. Encourage participation in your inservice workshops.
3. Offer to introduce reference materials to classes by using commercially prepared programs such as those offered with the purchase of NewsBank®, *World Almanac*, and *Encyclopedia Britannica*.
4. Accept as part of the media center staff's responsibility the "troubleshooting" of problems with equipment used in the classroom.

Make your equipment scheduling procedures WORK! Show the faculty that your system is reliable and that they can count on the equipment to work when they receive it. Catalog all materials for easy access and shelve them promptly and accurately. Additional access tools, such as a book catalog of audiovisual materials prepared in both title and subject format and kept at the circulation desk, will speed up the locational process.

This may seem like a very difficult service to perform. Actually, the procedures conform to those we are all used to following in relation to print resources and services. Our own perception of the importance and value of audiovisual materials in the learning process is the key element. If we are convinced, then we can convince others.

February

*"The frost performs its secret ministry,
unhelped by any wind."*

Samuel Taylor Coleridge
Frost at Midnight

February Birthdays

1564	Christopher Marlowe
1633	Samuel Pepys
1775	Charles Lamb
1807	Henry Wadsworth Longfellow
1809	Charles Darwin
1812	Charles Dickens
1828	Jules Verne
1874	Gertrude Stein
1882	James Joyce
1885	Sinclair Lewis
1886	William Rose Benét
1892	Edna St. Vincent Millay
1902	John Steinbeck
1902	Langston Hughes
1907	W. H. Auden
1907	James Michener
1912	Andre Norton
1914	Frank Bonham
1917	Carson McCullers
1917	Anthony Burgess
1926	Richard Matheson
1928	Robert Newton Peck
1929	Chaim Potok
1929	Len Deighton
1931	Toni Morrison
1937	Joanna Russ
1938	Judy Blume
1939	Jane Yolen
1942	Jamake Highwater
1942	Cynthia Voigt
1944	Alice Walker

MANAGEMENT TASKS

But, for true need —
You heavens, give me that patience,
patience I need!

William Shakespeare
King Lear

The management tasks I propose for your consideration in February are:

1. Automating procedures
2. Previewing materials

Automating Procedures

As of this writing, CO/ROM, or "Compact Disk/Read Only Memory," is the "new" method of data storage and retrieval. A year ago, it was a relatively little-known phenomenon. A large computer manufacturer has announced recently a revolutionary improvement in its product, making its current models virtually obsolete. I am sure you grasp my point. The journey toward automation of one's media center procedures and services seems more than a little like navigating one's way through a channel strewn with mines. The journey will be, quite literally, full of surprises, some costly, others less dangerous, but nevertheless impeding one's progress.

It is essential today that our educational programs equip students to understand the wide scope and potential of computer technology and to apply computer skills to the learning process. Although often in schools, the media centers are neglected as the administration plans computer programs, we should be among the first areas to be automated. We are coping with many management tasks that can be done profitably with computers, and, even more importantly, we are teaching information retrieval skills to students who will move out of our schools into a world where computers will provide the most common vehicle for accessing data.

School library/media centers are not entities unto themselves. They are components of the total school program, performing a function of integration with the school community and serving as a vital link, through technology, to the world outside the school. While televisions have become more common, in many schools computers in the media center are still uncommon. Sooner or later, as the media specialist in a secondary school, you *will* incorporate computer technology into your program.

Basically, the implementation of computer technology in your media center can have an impact on the way you retrieve information in reference activities, the way you manage administrative data, and the way you instruct students.

How can you navigate your journey through the mine field of automation with the fewest casualties?

First, do not try to make the journey alone. Seek advice from teachers and administrators already using computers, get in touch with other media specialists, seek out computer specialists in the district and in regional educational agencies, and attend conferences and workshops which will provide the information and awareness you need. Through contacts such as these, and through reading, you can equip yourself with a background in the "state-of-the-art" of computer technology.

Second, select the venture which will be your primary target: Information retrieval for reference activities, data management of your records, or instructional programs related to library/media skills. Your staff and their expertise, the funds available, and the professional time you can commit to automation will all affect your decisions. It is an illusion that computers save time; at least in the start-up phase, a great deal of time is needed to learn the processes and adapt them to your needs. Your staff will need inservice training.

Start with a modest proposal, since even a simple procedure will become complicated before you have it operating smoothly.

Once you have decided what you want to use a computer for, find software that will do the task. Then purchase the equipment which will accommodate the software. Or explain to computer company representatives what it is you want to accomplish, and let them find the software and hardware for you that will do exactly what you have specified.

Select equipment with an eye on the future. What kind of storage capability will be required as your needs increase and you expand your services? What new functions will the equipment handle? Will sharing of equipment be an aspect of your use? What quality do you want in your printouts?

Listed below are criteria you may wish to apply as you select tasks and services to automate:

- Is the task repetitive?
- Is the task boring?
- Does the information require updating?
- Is there an accounting function associated with the procedure?
- Are new sources of information needed?
- Is cross-reference access critical?
- Does the task require writing?
- Is speed of information retrieval critical?

As you prepare to automate certain procedures, keep these guidelines in mind:

1. Develop your plans with others in the school community, not in isolation.
2. Be very clear about what you want to do before purchasing software equipment.
3. Consider the need for inservice time.
4. Opt for simplicity.
5. Plan for the possibility of expansion.
6. Consider the space requirements of the new operation.

Previewing Materials

Most vendors of educational materials, both print and non-print, offer preview services to their customers. Some book publishers will send groups of books out for you to look over and select from. Conferences and publishers' exhibits also offer opportunities for examination of materials before purchase.

Under ideal conditions, we would include previewing in the selection of all the materials we purchase with taxpayers' money. In reality, this is not possible, and we rely on our standard selection tools, reviews from reputable sources, and the recommendations of others.

February is not too early to start your selection process for the new budget year and to plan for previewing as many of the materials as possible.

Your business administrator may permit the ordering of materials on preview by regular purchase order only. His or her concern is to be assured there is money encumbered for the material should it be lost or damaged and therefore not returnable. Although this makes the procedure a bit more complicated, it makes good sense.

If you order materials by purchase order rather than a simple letter or card of request, be careful to add this notation to the order: **FOR PREVIEW**. The company will then send you instructions, and often mailing labels, for return of the materials.

Most preview periods are for thirty days; to keep the material longer will result in a billing to the business office.

As materials arrive, note the arrival date and the date for return shipment on the packing slip and on your calendar.

Next, notify the person recommending the purchase, or the supervisor of the curriculum area for which it was selected. That person may wish to preview the material in the media center and should be able to arrange for that at his or her convenience. Some teachers like to preview material by using it with their classes; indeed, there are companies which urge this method for evaluation.

It is important for you to maintain control of the preview process, assuring that the material is returned to the vendor on time and in good condition.

You will want to reserve time to preview the material yourself. If you can establish a relatively quiet station for previewing, equipped with the machines needed, you will be able to expedite the procedure for yourself and others.

When the material is routed to staff, provide each previewer with an evaluation sheet, such as the one included in this book. As the close of the preview period draws near, you may find it necessary to send out a reminder. A form for doing so is also provided.

If your decision is to purchase the material, you may simply send the appropriate copy of the purchase order to the business office for payment. If you choose to return the material:

1. Return it to the vendor in the original packing.

2. Include a letter explaining the return. (A form letter for this purpose is included in the Appendix.)

3. Return the material according to the vendor's instructions.

4. ALWAYS INSURE.

Keep a copy in a file of each evaluation you receive whether the material is purchased or returned. Such information will be helpful should you decide to purchase at a later date. If the material is added to your collection the evaluations are useful as you recommend the title to other persons on staff.

LIBRARY RESEARCH PLANS

Level I: Human Physiology

The objectives for this library research plan are as follows:

- The students will review use of personal names as subject entries to the card catalog and periodical indexes.
- The students will be introduced to general biographical reference books in the media center.
- The students will learn about selected resources in the field of science.
- The students will read for specific information about a famous scientist.
- The students will take notes on their reading in the form of a brief biographical sketch.

Make copies of Figures 6-1 and 6-2 and distribute them to your students.

Level II: American Authors

The following are the objectives for this library research plan:

- The students will retrieve information about a specific author in media center resources.
- The students will reinforce locational skills using the card catalog and periodical index.
- The students will be introduced to the literary sources on microfiche.
- The students will use the indexes to encyclopedias.
- The students will learn to present written bibliographic citations.
- The students will communicate the information they have found in a written report.

Make copies of Figure 6-3, and distribute them to your students.

Level III: Outlining

The objectives for this library research plan are as follows:

- The students will learn the basic functions of a research outline.
- The students will learn an acceptable form for an outline.
- The students will present their research ideas and information in outline form.

Make copies of Figures 6-4 and 6-5, and distribute them to your students.

Name _____   Class _____

Date _____

HUMAN PHYSIOLOGY GUIDE

Here are several reference books which will be useful in completing your physiology assignment. These are general biographical reference sources:

Call Number   **Title**

_____   _____

_____   _____

_____   _____

_____   _____

Additionally, you will find these science references materials helpful:

_____   _____

_____   _____

_____   _____

Using the names of the scientists as subjects, continue your research in:

The card catalog

The Readers' Guide to Periodical Literature

_____

_____

Name _____ Class _____

Date _____

BIOGRAPHICAL SKETCH OF A FAMOUS PHYSIOLOGIST   6–2

Sign your name next to one of these famous physiologists. Then on a 5″ × 8″ index card, describe the contribution(s) made to the field of anatomy and/or physiology by that physiologist.

Your media specialist will have a copy of this list. Be sure to seek help in finding material if you have difficulty with this assignment.

DATE DUE _____

_____ Gasparo Aselli

_____ Frederick G. Banting

_____ W. M. Bayliss

_____ William Beaumont

_____ Claude Bernard

_____ C. H. Best

_____ Emil Du Bois-Reymond

_____ Paul Ehrlich

_____ Christiaan Eijkman

_____ Galen

_____ Robert A. Good

_____ John Haldane

_____ William Harvey

_____ Archibald V. Hill

_____ Andrew Fielding Huxley

_____ F. J. Julian

_____ Robert Koch

_____ Hans A. Krebs

6–2 cont'd.

_____ Karl Landsteiner

_____ Fritz A. Lipmann

_____ Otto Loewi

_____ Marcello Malpighi

_____ Élie Metchnikoff

_____ Otto Meyerhof

_____ Ivan P. Pavlov

_____ Réaumur

_____ Frederick Sanger

_____ Charles Sherrington

_____ Lazarro Spallanzani

_____ E. H. Starling

_____ Earl Sutherland

_____ Andreas Vesalius

_____ Albrecht Von Haller

_____

_____

ASSIGNMENT FOR AMERICAN AUTHORS 6–3

Author: _____

1. Choose three reference sources. Remember that you may use your textbook as one. Other sources are:
   - The card catalog (your author's name is a subject)
   - Vertical file (located through the card catalog)
   - *Who Was Who in America*
   - *Current Biography*
   - *Readers' Guide to Periodical Literature* (magazine articles are listed; request specific magazine at the circulation desk)
   - *New York Times on Microfiche* (fiche and indexes in binders)
   - NewsBank® (articles are from many newspapers; index is located with the microfiche)
   - Encyclopedias (use index in each volume, or the master index provided in final volume)
   - Use subject heading AMERICAN LITERATURE—HISTORY AND CRITICISM to locate other references

2. For each source, copy the following information:
   - Author or editor
   - Title
   - Publisher
   - Place of publication
   - Date of publication

3. Copy factual information (dates of birth and death; educational background; family information, if it is important to author's fame; literary history; interesting facts about author's life)

4. Compile this information from your three sources into a report which would be informative and interesting to the class. It should be about 150 words.

5. Make sure you list the three sources in the proper bibliographic form.

6. This finished paper is due _____.

6–4   **OUTLINING ASSIGNMENT**

Your assignment is as follows:

1. Study the notes you have taken as you researched your topic in the media center.

2. Read the guide to outlining that your media specialist has available.

3. Organize your ideas, thoughts, facts, and other information into the outline format presented in the guide.

4. Ask for assistance from your teacher and/or media specialist if necessary.

5. Rearrange the headings and subheadings of your outline, if necessary, to achieve a logical development of your ideas for your final report.

6. Submit your outline to the teacher for approval before starting to write your report.

Your outline is due on _____ .

OUTLINING GUIDE 6–5

When preparing to develop research notes into a research paper, you will find it helpful to put your ideas into outline form. This procedure will serve as a way of organizing your thoughts into a logical sequence before you attempt to write them in sentences and paragraphs.

The following is an acceptable format for an outline.

STATEMENT OF RESEARCH TOPIC _____

_____

_____

I. _____

_____

   A. _____

_____

      1. _____

      2. _____

_____

   B. _____

_____

      1. _____

      2. _____

_____

II. _____

_____

   AND SO ON

_____

_____

Your outline headings and subheadings may be expressed as either topics or as sentences. For example:

Topical heading: Legal aspects of hazardous waste disposal

Sentence heading: There are legal aspects to hazardous waste disposal.

Topic headings and sentence headings should not be used interchangeably in one outline.

An outline will state your ideas as main headings and will define and develop those ideas in the subheadings.

Important points to remember about an outline are:

1. It is the framework of your paper.

2. It should allow you to organize your information in a logical manner.

3. An outline should be brief. One page should be sufficient.

4. Once presented in the heading/subheading format, your outline can be revised to achieve the proper development of your research question.

FEBRUARY BULLETIN BOARDS

National Freedom Day
Washington's Birthday
Lincoln's Birthday
Groundhog Day
Black History Month
Leap Year
Foreign Language Week
National Inventors' Day
Valentine's Day
Music Month
Heart Month

How Do I Love Thee?

For the first half of the month of February, devote your bulletin board to hearts and messages of love. Scatter red hearts of varying sizes against a white background. Link them together with swirled lengths of pink crepe paper or ribbon.

Attach your caption: "How Do I Love Thee?" to the top of the bulletin board. Answer that question in one of two ways: Humorous verses from Valentines or literary quotations. Copy your selections in script onto rectangular strips of pink construction paper. Or, if possible, produce your quotes on the computer with an appropriate print.

To produce this simple bulletin board display will require:

- White and red construction paper
- Pink crepe paper or ribbon

Black History and Heroes

After February 14, you may want to change your display. If you should choose the theme "Black History," there are a number of ways you can approach it. Your objective could be to emphasize the positive, illustrating progress and the achievements of Black Americans.

Your title could be "Black Firsts," "Black Women," or "Black History—A Chronology." I recommend to you this source for information on these topics: *The Negro Almanac. A Reference Work on the Afro-American*, a Wiley-Interscience Publication, published by John Wiley and Sons. Do your research in the latest edition. You will find a chronology of historical events, a section on black "firsts," and a section about black women, as well as a great deal of other fascinating and informative subject matter.

As a background for the data you choose to present, compile a collage of appropriate pictures against a white background. Discarded newspapers and magazines are good sources for these pictures. The discarded monthly issues of *Current Biography*, as well as general interest publications, will provide pictures of famous blacks. You may want to keep the illustrations in black and white. Some photocopiers make clear illustrations in black and white from magazines and newspapers.

For this display you will need:

- White and black construction paper
- Black letters for your caption

Print your data in black on white construction paper and arrange it against the collage of pictures.

INSERVICE AND PUBLIC RELATIONS: EVALUATING SERVICES AND THE COLLECTION

Is it possible to know where you are going if you don't know where you are? Not likely. You will have intuitive feelings about your media program by February, the halfway point of the school year. However, it is important to obtain real data in order to evaluate your goals and objectives, to document the use of the media center and your media services, to be accountable for the manner in which you have allocated funds, and to evaluate the performance of yourself and your staff.

Devising an evaluation survey which will elicit the kinds of responses which are meaningful is a difficult task. There are many instruments available, designed by experts, which you can use or adapt to your needs. You will find such information in library management literature, or you will find that other media specialists in your district or region will be willing to share surveys they have devised and used.

Not all media services are appropriate, of course, for all school media centers. We have emphasized before that your program should function within the discrete educational program of your school. The program you are implementing throughout the year is a product of your planning and your effort to serve the school community effectively.

It is possible, as a first evaluation effort, to elicit teachers' and students' responses to a set of broad statements about staff, resources, and services. You will find that the results of such a survey will then form the basis for a follow-up questionnaire dealing with specifics.

There are four evaluation instruments presented in this chapter for your consideration. Two are designed for dissemination to staff and two for dissemination to a sample of students.

If you adapt these instruments to your situation, keep in mind that they should:

- be as brief as possible
- allow for anonymity
- be easy to score

The results of the first surveys will suggest the topics you should address in the follow-up surveys.

Prepare yourself for negative responses, and keep an objective viewpoint. Your survey may be the first opportunity dissatisfied, or disgruntled, users have had to articulate their complaints. Their responses may be based upon misinformation, or upon one unhappy experience in the media center. You will want to consider all responses carefully, and with your staff, identify the problems and address them.

Profile sheets are provided for recording the responses to the surveys that are presented, should you choose to use them without adaptation. These profiles allow you to see strengths and weaknesses at a glance.

Evaluation of program has been included as a part of public relations. Should you survey staff and student attitudes, and I strongly recommend this activity, you will realize an important by-product. Through this process, you will be communicating to your respondents about many facets of your program they may have missed. You will be achieving one of the objectives inherent to every good media program, that of creating awareness of staff, resources, and services.

To: Staff   Date _____
From: Media Center

MEDIA PROGRAM EVALUATION

Will you please assist us in this evaluation by taking a few moments to fill out this questionnaire? Sign

your response only if you want to. Return it to the media center by _____.

    Listed below are facets of school media programs which are generally accepted as desirable. Please indicate on a scale of 1 to 5 the extent to which you believe our program meets these criteria.

        1 = "missing"
        5 = "present to the most satisfactory degree"

A. STAFF

_____ Is knowledgeable in providing access to information.

_____ Has respect for individual needs of teachers and students.

_____ Is skillful in teaching research skills.

_____ Selects materials that are appropriate for our school.

_____ Administers a well organized and attractive media center.

_____ Works effectively and cooperatively with teachers.

_____ Is skillful in the production of non-print materials.

_____ Is available for individual and group inservice as needed.

B. RESOURCES

_____ Sufficient books are available in the media center.

_____ Sufficient audiovisual materials are available.

_____ The book selection supports recreational reading.

_____ The periodical collection is useful for student research.

_____ The reference collection supports student research.

_____ Adequate AV equipment is available for my use.

_____ The equipment is repaired satisfactorily.

_____ It is easy to locate materials in the media center.

_____ The media center collection of resources is up to date.

cont'd.

C. PROGRAM

_____ Students and staff are encouraged to read for pleasure.

_____ The atmosphere in the media center attracts students.

_____ Instruction in library/media use is available to students.

_____ Skills instruction meets the needs of my students.

_____ Students learn to work independently in the media center.

_____ I am informed regarding media center services and resources.

_____ I can participate in selection by previewing materials.

_____ The production of materials assists me in my teaching.

_____ Access to materials from other libraries is available.

_____ Professional materials are available for staff development.

_____ Bibliographies are provided to assist me in my teaching.

_____ The established loan procedures are appropriate.

_____ The media center program supplements the curriculum.

D. SUGGESTIONS

_____

_____

_____

_____

_____

_____

_____

Your suggestions for improving media center services and programs will be appreciated. Thank you!

Student Evaluation of Media Program Date _____
Profile of Responses

Count responses in each of the five categories. Record the number in the appropriate box. Draw an "X" over the box where the median response falls. Draw a line joining boxes marked with "X's." Turn the profile lengthwise to see variations in responses to complete questionnaire.

A. STAFF

	5	4	3	2	1
Is knowledgeable in obtaining information					
Has respect for individual needs					
Teaches research skills skillfully					
Selects appropriate materials					
Maintains organized, attractive center					
Effective and cooperative with students					
Skillful in producing AV materials					
Available for individual or group help					

B. RESOURCES

Books in collection are sufficient					
Audiovisual materials are sufficient					
Books are available for leisure reading					
Periodical collection is useful					
Reference collection supports research					
AV equipment is adequately available					
Repair of equipment is satisfactory					
Materials can be located easily					
The media center resources are up to date					

C. PROGRAM

Reading for pleasure is encouraged					
Atmosphere of media center attracts students					
Media skills instruction is available					
Skills instruction meets students' needs					
Students work independently in the media center					
Students are informed about services resources					
Students help select materials					
Media production assists in studies					
Interlibrary loan is available					
Extra-curricular materials are available					
Bibliographies help find materials					
Loan procedures are appropriate					
Media program supplements the curriculum					

D. SUGGESTIONS

_____

_____

_____

To: Students
From: Media Center

Date _____

MEDIA PROGRAM EVALUATION

Will you please assist us in this evaluation by taking a few moments to fill out this questionnaire? Sign your response only if you want to. Return it to the media center by _____.

Listed below are facets of school media programs which are generally accepted as desirable. Please indicate on a scale of 1 to 5 the extent to which you believe our program meets these criteria.

1 = "missing"
5 = "present to the most satisfactory degree"

A. STAFF

_____ Is knowledgeable in providing access to information.

_____ Has respect for individual needs of students.

_____ Is skillful in teaching research skills.

_____ Selects materials that are appropriate for my research.

_____ Administers a well organized and attractive media center.

_____ Works effectively and cooperatively with students.

_____ Is skillful in the production of nonprint materials.

_____ Is available for individual and group help as needed.

B. RESOURCES

_____ Sufficient books are available in the media center.

_____ Sufficient audiovisual materials are available.

_____ The book selection supports recreational reading.

_____ The periodical collection is useful for my research.

_____ The reference collection supports student research.

_____ Adequate AV equipment is available for my use.

_____ The equipment works satisfactorily.

_____ It is easy to locate materials in the media center.

_____ The media center collection of resources is up to date.

To: Staff
From: Media Center

Date _____

cont'd.

C. PROGRAM

_____ Students are encouraged to read for pleasure.

_____ The atmosphere in the media center attracts students.

_____ Instruction in library/media use is available to students.

_____ Skills instruction meets my needs.

_____ Students learn to work independently in the media center.

_____ I am informed regarding media center services and resources.

_____ I can participate in selection of library materials.

_____ The production of materials assists me in my studies.

_____ Access to materials from other libraries is available.

_____ Materials are available for extra-curricular interests.

_____ Bibliographies are provided to help me choose materials.

_____ The established loan procedures are appropriate.

_____ The media center program supplements the curriculum.

D. SUGGESTIONS

_____

_____

_____

_____

_____

_____

_____

_____

Your suggestions for improving media center services and programs will be appreciated. Thank you!

Staff Evaluation of Media Program   Date _____
Profile of Responses

Count responses in each of the five categories. Record the number in the appropriate box. Draw an
"X" over the box where the median response falls. Draw a line joining boxes marked with "X's."
Turn the profile lengthwise to see variations in responses to complete questionnaire.

A. STAFF:

	5	4	3	2	1
Is knowledgeable in obtaining information					
Has respect for individual needs					
Teaches research skills skillfully					
Selects appropriate materials					
Maintains organized, attractive center					
Effective and cooperative with teachers					
Skillful in producing AV materials					
Available for individual or group inservice					

B. RESOURCES:

Books in collection are sufficient					
Audiovisual materials are sufficient					
Books are available for leisure reading					
Periodical collection is useful					
Reference collection supports research					
AV equipment is adequately available					
Repair of equipment is satisfactory					
Materials can be located easily					
The media center resources are up to date					

C. PROGRAM:

Reading for pleasure is encouraged					
Atmosphere of media center attracts students					
Media skills instruction is available					
Skills instruction meets students' needs					
Students work independently in the media center					
Staff are informed about services/resources					
Previewing helps me to select materials					
Media production assists in teaching					
Interlibrary loan is available					
Professional materials are available					
Bibliographies are prepared for teachers					
Loan procedures are appropriate					
Media program supplements the curriculum					

D. SUGGESTIONS:

_____

_____

_____

_____

To: Staff

From: Media Center

Date _____

SURVEY OF MEDIA CENTER USE

Please help us evaluate media center use by answering the following questionnaire. For purposes of this survey the following key should be used:

(O) Often = Once a week or more
(R) Regularly = Once or twice a month
(S) Sometimes = Once or twice a semester
(N) Never = Never

	O	R	S	N
1. To complete my assignments my students need to use media center resources	☐	☐	☐	☐
2. I schedule my classes into the media center	☐	☐	☐	☐
3. My assignments call for use of the following resources:				
Current news (daily papers)	☐	☐	☐	☐
Facts-on-File	☐	☐	☐	☐
Magazines	☐	☐	☐	☐
Reference books	☐	☐	☐	☐
Vertical files (pamphlets, etc.)	☐	☐	☐	☐
Audiovisual materials	☐	☐	☐	☐
Interlibrary loan	☐	☐	☐	☐
Computer programs	☐	☐	☐	☐
Fiction books	☐	☐	☐	☐
High interest/low reading level books	☐	☐	☐	☐
Encyclopedias	☐	☐	☐	☐
SIRS	☐	☐	☐	☐
_____	☐	☐	☐	☐
_____	☐	☐	☐	☐
4. In the classroom, in class preparation, and personally, I use:	☐	☐	☐	☐
Bibliographies	☐	☐	☐	☐
Publishers' catalogs	☐	☐	☐	☐
Professional books and magazines	☐	☐	☐	☐
Periodical routing service	☐	☐	☐	☐
Video playback	☐	☐	☐	☐
Audiovisual materials & equipment	☐	☐	☐	☐
ERIC searches	☐	☐	☐	☐
Previewing service	☐	☐	☐	☐
Fiction books	☐	☐	☐	☐
Current news services	☐	☐	☐	☐

5. I would like to see the media center purchase the following:

_____

_____

_____

Date _____

SURVEY OF MEDIA CENTER USE

Please help us evaluate media center use by answering the following questionnaire. For purposes of this survey the following key should be used:

(O) Often = Once a week or more
(R) Regularly = Once or twice a month
(S) Sometimes = Once or twice a semester
(N) Never = Never

	O	R	S	N
1. To complete my assignments I use media center resources	☐	☐	☐	☐
2. My classes are scheduled into the media center	☐	☐	☐	☐

3. My assignments call for use of the following resources:

	O	R	S	N
Current news (daily papers)	☐	☐	☐	☐
Facts-on-File	☐	☐	☐	☐
Magazines	☐	☐	☐	☐
Reference books	☐	☐	☐	☐
Vertical files (pamphlets, etc.)	☐	☐	☐	☐
Audiovisual materials	☐	☐	☐	☐
Interlibrary loan	☐	☐	☐	☐
Computer programs	☐	☐	☐	☐
Fiction books	☐	☐	☐	☐
High interest/low reading level books	☐	☐	☐	☐
Encyclopedias	☐	☐	☐	☐
SIRS	☐	☐	☐	☐
_____	☐	☐	☐	☐
_____	☐	☐	☐	☐

4. During free time I use the media center to:

	O	R	S	N
Read newspapers	☐	☐	☐	☐
Read magazines	☐	☐	☐	☐
Do my homework	☐	☐	☐	☐
Use audiovisual materials	☐	☐	☐	☐
Read fiction	☐	☐	☐	☐
Talk with friends	☐	☐	☐	☐
Use the computers	☐	☐	☐	☐
Read non-fiction books	☐	☐	☐	☐
Research	☐	☐	☐	☐

5. I would like to see the media center purchase the following:

_____

_____

_____

March

"...daffodils,
That come before the swallow dares, and take
The winds of March with beauty..."

William Shakespeare
The Winter's Tale

March Birthdays

1806	Elizabeth Barrett Browning
1809	Nikolai Gogol
1828	Henrik Ibsen
1870	Frank Norris
1874	Robert Frost
1880	Sean O'Casey
1885	Ring Lardner
1911	Tennessee Williams
1914	Ralph Ellison
1922	Jack Kerouac
1924	Herbert Gold
1925	Flannery O'Connor
1926	John Fowles
1928	Alan Sillitoe
1932	John Updike
1933	Philip Roth
1934	Zibby Oneal
1936	Judith Guest
1942	John Irving

MANAGEMENT TASKS

---

*"Trust thyself; every heart
vibrates to that iron string."*

Ralph Waldo Emerson
Self-Reliance

The management tasks for March are:

1. Maintaining equipment
2. Sharing resources

Maintaining Equipment

An important function of your media program, if equipment is housed and dispatched from your facility, is the task of keeping that equipment in good working order. Many teachers and administrators are uncomfortable using audiovisual equipment in the first place, and, if they experience poor performance from the machines you provide, their anxieties are heightened tenfold. In order to achieve success with a lesson that includes audiovisuals, a teacher must:

- Have selected the appropriate materials
- Be familiar with the content
- Prepare the class for the lesson
- Be experienced in operating the equipment
- Use the equipment in the proper setting
- Be provided with equipment that performs satisfactorily

You, as the media specialist, can affect the outcome of the lesson, because you provide services which have a direct bearing on several of these variables.

Through involvement in lesson planning, you help the teacher select the right material for the lesson, and you provide a place for previewing of that material. You offer inservice for anyone needing assistance in equipment operation. Responsibility for the successful use of audiovisuals in the classroom extends beyond delivery of the requested equipment. You must be sure that the equipment functions for the teacher's purposes.

A great deal of equipment maintenance is a matter of common sense, good organization, and consistency of procedure. Within your media center facility, you should establish an area for equipment maintenance. This area should be secure and should include these basics:

- Tools for minor repair, including a film splicer
- Easy egress to halls and elevators
- Secure storage for lamps and parts such as cords, cables, three-prong adaptors
- A workbench equipped with electrical power

Where equipment is concerned, regular cleaning is essential. Those persons with responsibility for delivering and picking up equipment should follow these procedures routinely:

132

1. Retract cords before moving equipment.
2. Return equipment to stable position on cart before moving it.
3. Wipe lenses and surfaces regularly, according to the manufacturers' instructions regarding solutions and materials.
4. Attach spare lamps to equipment and carts before delivering them.
5. Include adaptors where needed.
6. Make sure operating instructions are intact.
7. Replace covers on equipment if it is to be stored for more than a day or two.

Your responsibilities for repairing equipment should not extend beyond simple adjustment of mechanisms, limited cleaning, and changing lamps. Above all, do not assume responsibility for sophisticated equipment such as VCRs, cameras, or computers. We suggested in a previous chapter that you establish channels for equipment repair. Generally, this is done at the district level, but if you are allowed to select the service company, do so with these factors in mind:

- Promptness of service
- Hourly labor costs
- Reputation
- Guarantee of work
- Willingness to estimate costs ahead of time
- Transportation of equipment

Maintain a good relationship with your service company as well as with the dealers from whom the equipment has been purchased. It is often possible to solve a minor problem by getting advice over the telephone.

All operating manuals, schematics, repair records, guaranties and warranties should be filed for easy access. Making photocopies of these important documents is advised. Because it is likely there will be frequent handling of these documents, it is helpful to have them laminated.

Sharing Resources

The scope of resources and services the students and teachers in your school require and expect expands with each new course added to the curriculum, with every revised state syllabus, with all new expectations of our educational systems, and with advanced technologies for learning in school and during a lifetime of continuing education.

Individual school library/media center programs can no longer go it alone, trying to provide the materials and services that are needed. It is necessary to tap into every additional source available, to connect with other institutions, information banks, libraries, and agencies that can provide the access to resources you lack.

To be able to take advantage of other sources, one must be philosophically ready to share one's own resources. On the surface, this would appear to present no problem. As media specialists, we realize a sense of satisfaction when we serve as the catalyst between people and their informational needs, and we continually strive for that end. However, the staff—including the administrators—of your school may be happy to be on the receiving end of resource-sharing, but chary of any program that releases their media materials to persons or agencies outside the school.

Your first task may be one of communicating the benefits of "networking" or "resource sharing" to your staff. Some of the materials and services which would enhance your program need to be outlined for them:

1. Union catalogs can provide access to additional sources.
2. Bibliographic searches can provide information for teachers and students alike.
3. Professional cataloging assistance can be available for faster and more accurate maintenance of the school's collection.
4. Interlibrary loan adds wider scope of materials for use in the school.
5. Cooperative collection development allows for valid planning and the building of special collections.

Resource sharing can start modestly within the district. If the media specialists in your district are ready to share, their first step should be to compile a district union list of holdings. Such a list will provide very desirable sharing among the centers and will give you an opportunity to design a collection development plan, which will avoid costly duplication of materials.

As a group, you should formulate loan policies and then conscientiously adhere to them. You will need to respect the fact that one's own faculty and students will necessarily come first when considering the loan of materials. Most districts have interschool delivery systems which can be used for getting the materials around.

Charity does, indeed, begin at home, and once you have discovered that a process of sharing within the district will work and effectively improve your collections and services, you are ready to investigate the possibilities of doing the same with other schools, public libraries, information networks, and agencies.

Sophisticated systems for resource sharing are in place for many schools. In some cases, your district may pay a fee to belong to a system of school libraries. As you look into the various opportunities available to you, keep these procedural questions in mind:

- Is there provision for reimbursement in case of loss?
- Can delivery be accomplished in a timely fashion?
- Are there professionals directing the effort?
- Are adequate records required for the transactions?
- Do the procedures allow for updating lists?

All of us can benefit from sharing whether our collections are large or small, our services many or few. It is the spirit of cooperation that makes networking successful.

LIBRARY RESEARCH PLANS

Level I: Housing

The objectives for this library research plan are as follows:

- The students will accomplish research in a wide variety of sources in the media center.
- The students will gain experience in the following research skills: (1) using indexes to material, (2) using the card catalog, (3) finding sources in periodical indexes, (4) using current news sources, and (5) using SIRS and the vertical file.
- The students will report on their research and present the sources in correct bibliographic form.

Make copies of Figures 7-1 and 7-2 and distribute them to your students.

Level II: Social Psychology

The objectives for this library research plan are as follows:

- The students will use *The Readers' Guide to Periodical Literature* to find an article about an assigned topic.
- The students will read the article for understanding.
- The students will learn what a "précis" is.
- The students will write a précis of the article they have read.
- The students will gain skill in reading for comprehension.

Make copies of Figures 7–3 and 7–4, and distribute them to your students.

Level III: American Novel

The objectives for this library research plan are as follows:

- The students will use reserve materials in the media center to research an ethnic group.
- The students will use subject entries to a variety of additional resources in the media center.
- The students will read a fiction book and relate the story to the theme of the ethnological development of America.
- The students will gain experience in taking notes.
- The students will communicate their ideas in written form, using correct bibliographic style.

Make copies of Figures 7-5 and 7-6 and distribute them to your students.

7–1   **GUIDE FOR HOUSING**

To complete this series of assignments about housing, you will need to use many different sources in the media center. Here are a few places to start:

The card catalog
The Readers' Guide to Periodical Literature
SIRS
National Geographic Index
Encyclopedias
NewsBank®

_____

_____

_____

A few subject headings you should use as you research these materials are:

Civilization, Primitive
Man, Primitive
Housing
Architecture
Interior Decoration
U.S. History—Social Life and Customs
Occupations
Interior Design as a Profession

_____

_____

_____

The media center has a few audiovisual programs related to the topics in this assignment. These can be located through the card catalog.

Good luck! Do not hesitate to ask for assistance.

Name _____ Class _____

Date _____

PROJECTS FOR HOUSING RESEARCH 7–2

You are required to use three different sources for each of the following assignments. Keep your bibliographic information on 3″ × 5″ index cards. Consult with the media specialist and use the guide to sources that has been prepared for you.

Assignment 1

Choose one prehistoric shelter. Research and describe how the housing was used, where, and how it was made. Include the customs or traditions that were related to its use. Make a drawing to illustrate the prehistoric shelter.

Date due: _____

Assignment 2

Choose a country and describe its predominant style of architecture. Tell how it has influenced American architecture.

Date due: _____

Assignment 3

Choose one architect and describe his or her style and influence on American architecture.

Date due: _____

Assignment 4

Select an era in American history and describe the times, events, and style of housing interiors that were popular at that time.

Date due: _____

Assignment 5

Check into a career related to housing interiors. Describe the duties of such a job, the schooling required, and the market for the jobs in that field.

Date due: _____

Assignment 6

Mobile homes are quite popular. Discuss why this is so. Describe the controversies in some communities regarding zoning have has positive or negative effects on this type of housing.

Date due: _____

7–3   GUIDE FOR SOCIAL PSYCHOLOGY

Writing a Précis of a Magazine Article

A précis is a brief summary of essential points; statements of facts.
For example:

Dapper, Martin. ''Grooming Your Dog,'' *Petting Pets*, Vol. 6, November 21, 1987.

Précis: The topics summarized in this article include the proper tools for dog grooming, steps to follow for the dog's grooming from the bath to the final touches, how to tell when grooming is needed, and where it should take place. The article concludes with specific suggestions for making the experience a pleasurable one for your dog.

SOCIAL PSYCHOLOGY ASSIGNMENT   7–4

This assignment is to be completed in the media center in one class period.

Step 1. Select a topic from this list:

     a. Parenting

     b. Developing a child's socialization skills

     c. Dealing with your child's handicap

     d. Missing children

     e. Developing a child's coordination

     f. Teaching a child about death

     g. Family Planning

     h. Preparing a child for a new sibling

Step 2. Find an article about your topic in the periodical guide.

Step 3. Follow the proper procedure for checking out the magazine.

Step 4. Read the article as many times as necessary to understand it fully.

Step 5. Write down a full bibliographic citation for the article.

Step 6. Return the magazine to the circulation desk.

Step 7. Write a précis of the article, including the bibliographic information. A guide is provided to help you.

Name _____ Class _____

Date _____

7–5　　　　GUIDE FOR AMERICAN NOVEL

A collection of books has been placed on reserve for your class. It is located _____.

These books may be used in the media center and checked out overnight. Please be responsible about returning them promptly.

In addition to the reserve materials, you may want to search further by using:

The card catalog

Readers' Guide to Periodical Literature

Microfiche program: *A Nation of Immigrants*

NewsBank®

Indexes to *American Heritage* and *Horizon*

New York Times Index and *New York Times Current Events on Microfiche*

The vertical file

_____

_____

Subject entries to these resources include:

IMMIGRATION AND EMIGRATION

CHILDREN OF IMMIGRANTS

ETHNIC GROUPS

MEXICAN AMERICANS (etc.)

UNITED STATES—HISTORY

UNITED STATES—SOCIAL LIFE AND CUSTOMS

Name _____   Class _____

Date _____

AMERICAN NOVEL ASSIGNMENT   7–6

Select either A or B to complete this assignment.

A. Research an ethnic group drawn from your own family's background. Why did this group come to the United States? What skills and culture did they bring with them? Did they achieve the "American Dream"?

B. Read a book dealing with the "American Dream," using one reference book to highlight the ethnic focus of the book. Here are some suggestions:

Ramona	*Down These Mean Streets*
American Hunger	*Evergreen*
Giants in the Earth	*Goodbye, Columbus*
The Last Hurrah	*Warrior Woman*
O Pioneers!	*China Men*

_____

_____

SPECIFICS FOR A AND B

1. There are books on reserve in the media center. For A, use three sources as a minimum, only one of which can be an encyclopedia. For B, use one reference source in addition to the book you select to read.

2. Take notes on 3″ × 5″ cards.

3. Make a plan for your paper and *then* write.

4. Your paper should be a minimum of 1500 words.

5. Doublespace whether typed or handwritten.

6. Use correct form for your footnotes and bibliography.

7. Your topic is due: _____.

8. Your paper is due: _____.

MARCH BULLETIN BOARDS

Ides of March
Foreign Language Week
Art Week
International Women's Day
Johnny Appleseed Day
World Meteorological Day
First Day of Spring
Procrastination Week
Women's History Week
Earth Day
St. Patrick's Day
Wildlife Week

For Your Career . . . Don't Trust Luck!

As you approach the final quarter of the school year many of the students in your school are planning next year's schedule of classes, choosing a college, starting to think about summer work, or, in some way, thinking about the future. Counselors are facilitating college conferences, and, in some schools, encouraging students to think about careers by spending a day on a particular job.

This is a good time to focus on the process of choosing a career, with emphasis upon the planning that this process should entail.

My suggestion for a bulletin board on this topic employs the techniques of enlarging illustrations with an overhead projector or an opaque projector.

First, visualize your bulletin board as two halves. One half will illustrate "luck," while the other will show "planning." The caption at the top of the board should spell out: FOR YOUR CAREER. . .

The left side of your board should have the caption: "DON'T TRUST LUCK!" The right side should be titled: "PLAN NOW!"

The "luck" side of the bulletin board should accommodate four or five symbols of luck, depending upon the size you make them. A similar number of enlarged photographs should be selected to illustrate "planning."

Suggestions for "luck" are: A shamrock, a pair of dice, a lottery ticket, a roulette wheel, a hand of cards, a crystal ball. Use the following techniques for producing these illustrations:

Overhead Projector

1. Make a photocopy of the illustration selected.

2. Make an overhead transparency from the paper copy.

3. Tape a large piece of white paper to the wall.

4. Project the transparency onto the paper, moving the projector until you have a projection which is the size you want.

5. Trace over the lines of the picture with a soft pencil.

6. Take the picture from the wall and complete it with markers or soft colored drawing pencils.

Opaque Projector

1. Place your selected illustration on the stage of the opaque projector.

2. Tape a large piece of white paper to the wall.

3. Project the image onto the paper, moving the projector until you have the picture size you want.

4. Trace the lines of the pictures.

5. Take the picture from the wall and complete it with markers or soft colored drawing pencils.

To illustrate ''planning'' take pictures of the following scenes and have them enlarged to eight-inch by ten-inch size: A student reading in your media center; a student viewing a videotape; a student using a computer (or a microform reader); a counselor conferring with a student; students listening to a speaker.

Your photographs will display more dramatically if you mount them on contrasting and varied construction paper. They should need no individual captions.

This bulletin board requires the following materials:

• Three-inch letters for the captions

• Photographs

• Construction paper for a background and for your illustrations

• Colored pencils or bold markers

INSERVICE AND PUBLIC RELATIONS: TIPS FOR TEACHERS

It is quite easy for us to assume that teachers are well-informed about use of libraries and the function of the school library/media center in the learning process. For us, after all, this is the name of the game. Library research skills spell success in school; the media center is central to the learning process.

Actually, teachers need our help in understanding how to go about using the resources of the media center most effectively. Often, a few suggestions, though they state what is obvious to us, can improve the manner in which the teacher assigns library-related activities, and once again you are conveying the message that you are a part of the educational team.

The following tips, when adapted to your situation, can be printed up for distribution to teachers who, experience now tells you, are making assignments which involve library use.

1. Assignments made without knowledge of library resources often prove difficult or impossible to implement. Student interest and initiative may be thwarted.

TIP: VISIT OUR LIBRARY FIRST. One of our staff will be glad to show you the materials in your field and to discuss your needs.

2. Giving several classes the same assignment at the same time engenders student frustration because materials are limited.

   TIP: TRY TO STAGGER MAJOR ASSIGNMENTS. Perhaps you will want to request limited circulation for materials. Within your department, you may be able to vary your lesson plans to avoid the problem of everyone teaching the same unit at once.

3. An entire class assigned to use one or two specific titles will not be able to find material.

   TIP: MAKE SURE THE MEDIA CENTER OWNS THE TITLES YOU ASSIGN. Let us put them on reserve for your class.

4. Mutilated newspapers and magazines and books from the reference and general collections are ruined for further use.

   TIP: PLEASE EMPHASIZE THAT LIBRARY MATERIALS MUST NOT BE CUT. If clippings are required for your assignment, inquire about discarded materials that we may have available for your students.

5. We may not have books with the most recent data on your assigned subjects.

   TIP: For current issues, encourage the use of magazines, *Facts-on-File*, newspapers, our news sources on microfiche, SIRS, pamphlets, and on-line data searches.

6. Assignments given orally are sometimes misunderstood.

   TIP: THE MEDIA CENTER WOULD APPRECIATE A COPY OF THE ASSIGNMENT.

7. Unauthorized circulation of reference books often results in loss of books.

   TIP: Please send a WRITTEN REQUEST with a student when you wish certain materials for the classroom.

8. Our staff requires time to prepare for class visits, to compile bibliographies, to prepare a book talk, and to collect materials for a reserve collection.

   TIP: ARRANGE FOR THESE SERVICES AT THE EARLIEST POSSIBLE TIME IN YOUR PLANS. We would like to be in on the planning, in fact.

9. Successful research assignments are often Social Studies/English or English/Science combinations.

   TIP: The English teacher can give credit for the mechanics; the Social Studies or Science teacher can grade for content. You may want to TEAM UP on library-related assignments.

10. Borrow new books, talk about them, and let students preview them.

TIP: The media center staff will bring NEW BOOKS to your classroom and publicize them if you would like us to.

11. Oral book reports can promote reading, sharpen listening and communication skills.

12. Encourage your students to consider audiovisual programs when doing research in the media center.

TIP: Audiovisual materials are cataloged and accessible through the card catalog. We have equipment for listening and viewing materials in the center.

13. When assigning research projects, encourage students to add audiovisual media to their presentations.

TIP: The media center staff can help students prepare video and audio tapes, slide programs, transparencies, computer graphics, and other non-traditional media.

14. The media staff is pleased to be invited to observe the results of library-related assignments.

TIP: Invite us to your panel discussions, book reports, and other culminating activities. We will accept!

April

"Strawe me the ground with daffadown dillies and cowslips, and kingcups, and loved lillies. . ."

Edmund Spenser
Aprill

April Birthdays

1564	William Shakespeare
1707	Henry Fielding
1770	William Wordsworth
1783	Washington Irving
1805	Hans Christian Andersen
1815	Anthony Trollope
1816	Charlotte Brontë
1840	Émile Zola
1843	Henry James
1896	Robert Sherwood
1897	Thornton Wilder
1899	Ngaio Marsh
1899	Vladimir Nabokov
1905	Robert Penn Warren
1906	Samuel Beckett
1909	Eudora Welty
1914	Bernard Malamud
1916	Beverly Cleary
1920	Arthur Hailey
1922	Kingsley Amis
1928	Cynthia Ozick
1931	Donald Barthelme
1934	Richard Peck

MANAGEMENT TASKS

"There is no new thing under the sun."

Ecclesiastes 1:9

The management tasks for April are:

1. Selecting and ordering materials
2. Producing nonprint instructional materials

Selecting and Ordering Materials

During the month of April the school calendar winds down into the final quarter of the year. Even though activities in the media center are brisk, with students and teachers concentrating on the extensive assignments that must be completed before the final grades are averaged, it is essential for you to select and prepare the orders for the materials you will purchase on the new budget. You will want those orders to be ready as soon as the business office will accept them so that the materials will arrive over the summer and be on hand for the opening of school in the fall.

By this time in the year, you have received suggestions from staff for purchases, and you have recognized the need for certain materials and noted them in your log. Your surveys in February may have yielded suggestions for purchase. Your inventory of the collection, which you will start in May, will reveal losses and weak areas that you will need to address in your selection process.

Does your school district have a policy statement regarding the selection of instructional materials? If the answer to this question is "No," you and the other media specialists in the district must develop one and present it to the Board of Education for approval. There are many examples of such statements to be found in library literature and you need not reinvent the wheel. Such a policy statement should set forth:

1. *The legal responsibility for the selection and approval of print and non-print materials used in the school district.* Generally, this is the Board of Education, as the governing body of the district.
2. *The objectives of selection.* These objectives should reflect general understandings of the goals of the total school program.
3. *The criteria for selection of materials.* This section of the policy should state clearly the qualities one looks for in materials selected for purchase with district funds.
4. *The methods used in selection procedures.* It is useful to state the standard selection tools and the methods employed in previewing and personally evaluating materials.
5. *The procedures that will be used to meet challenges to materials purchased for student use.* This should provide for designation of the person or persons who will consider any objections or complaints to materials. Providing a form for the reconsideration of challenged material will be helpful.

If you undertake the writing of a district-wide policy statement regarding materials selection, it will be important for you to involve the supervisors of the various disciplines.

148

The English supervisor already may have developed guidelines for his/her department; social studies and science supervisors should be interested also in the process, since they are often evaluating controversial materials.

Lacking an established policy statement for evaluation and selection of materials, you will do well to prepare for your staff a set of criteria. In writing them down, you will strengthen in your own mind your accountability for the expenditure of funds allocated to you. Referring to your list will keep you on track as you work through the tasks of selecting and ordering materials.

Your criteria for selection should include:

- Need
- Level of difficulty
- Diversity of opinion or point of view
- Artistic quality
- Appropriateness of format
- Accuracy and authority
- Cost
- Recommendations

Whenever possible, you should examine the material before ordering. Your preview procedures should help in this regard, especially with nonprint programs. Educational consortiums often arrange for book exhibits; most publishers will send materials for free examinations. All of these possibilities are time-consuming and you will find youself relying most often upon book reviews and the standard selection tools. If material proves unacceptable, when it arrives, you should never hesitate to send it back for credit with a simple note to the publisher indicating that it is not appropriate for your collection.

When you solicit recommendations for purchase from staff and students, ask them to present them on a form you provide. The more information they can provide, the easier it will be to complete the ordering procedure. As you make your selections, prepare the same form for each title.

Your procedure then for ordering should involve these steps:

1. Select purchases from recommendations.
2. Arrange forms alphabetically by title.
3. Check titles against your card catalog to avoid duplication.
4. Check titles in *Books In Print* or publishers' catalogs for full ordering information.
5. Prepare purchase orders.
6. File order forms for verification when order arrives.

Use jobbers whenever possible. When you select a jobber, prepare specifications for the processing of your materials and submit them with the order. Purchase as many items as possible fully processed. You will save time and money in the long run. Book jobbers now offer preparation of materials for your security system, also, and will offer you a record of your order in machine-readable form for entry into your computer-based circulation system and/or catalog.

Producers of audiovisual materials generally offer catalog card sets free with purchased materials. If you do not note such an offer in the catalog, add the request for cards to your purchase order.

Most publishers' catalogs will estimate shipping costs for you. Be sure to figure this amount into your purchase order or allow five percent of the total cost of the material for handling charges in your budget book.

Though you are starting this selection and ordering procedure—which is both critical and time-consuming—in May, it is not likely that your orders can be processed until the budget for the coming year is in place, and the business office is prepared to accept your orders.

Producing Nonprint Instructional Materials

As you, your staff, and the teachers in your building prepare recommendations for purchase of materials you will find that appropriate nonprint programs to enhance certain teaching units simply cannot be located. The answer to this problem can be the creation, in-house, of needed materials.

Several factors have an effect upon just how much media production can and should take place in your media center. You will not want to publicize and offer media production unless you are prepared, truly, to deliver the goods. The scope and content of your production service should be determined by the following conditions:

- The enthusiasm and expertise of the persons on your staff
- The willingness of the requesting teacher to contribute to the process
- The time all persons involved can devote to the production
- The equipment you have available
- The production supplies available
- The validity of the perceived need
- The extent of administrative support
- Space required for production

Everyone involved in media production for instructional use should understand at the outset that materials produced with district funds and during school time are the property of the school district. Full compliance with the copyrights of others must be assured, also. Materials simply cannot be "adapted" or "borrowed" and then used regularly in instruction.

If you, or some member of your staff, is skilled in media production, this service can be a tremendous benefit to your building and possibly your district. Your objectives in such a situation should be to improve your budget, supplies and facility in order to capitalize upon this highly desirable function.

However, even if you are lacking in the components that are necessary for the advanced media production, you still can offer certain limited services to teachers in this area. You possibly can do the following:

1. Record television programs off-air for permissible classroom use.

2. Videotape lectures, classroom activities, guest speakers, field trips, concerts and plays.

3. Audiotape lectures, guest speakers, musical performances.

4. Take the pictures for a slide presentation.

5. Audiotape sound for a slide presentation.

6. Prepare transparencies.

7. Photocopy materials.

8. Prepare graphics by computer.

9. Prepare photo images using a copy stand.

10. Laminate materials.

All of the activities listed above fall within the definition of media production, and yet, none requires skills beyond your abilities. They do require time and a willingness to experiment, as well as equipment and supplies. If the necessary equipment is unavailable in your center, you may find it located in other areas of the school. You may have to use the facilities in other areas. If you can demonstrate your willingness to offer media production to the staff, and they, in turn, demonstrate a desire to take advantage of such service, your goal should become one of establishing an area within your media center that is properly equipped.

When you prepare your budget, you should include the supply items needed for production. Whether you are prepared to offer media production or not, being able to supply certain materials to your teachers will enhance your image. The kinds of supply items they can use will include:

- Transparency markers (permanent and water soluble)

- Acetate for transparencies (sheets and rolls)

- Video and audio tapes

- Copier and computer paper and computer disks

- Slide mounts

- Film

Be as generous with supplies as your budget will allow. Assist teachers in learning the use of production equipment and allow them to use it in your facility or out. Purchase ''how-to'' books, manuals, and visuals for your collection.

Some of the teachers in your building may be skillful at designing and producing instructional materials. You can facilitate the process many times by putting them in touch with one another and by providing the tools for creating the materials they need.

Students, also, should be offered the opportunity to create nonprint materials to complete their assignments. If their teachers have not suggested alternatives to the usual written assignment, you can be prepared to do so. A research checklist, offered as the tool for the individual student to evaluate his research process, should include the suggestion that consideration be given to incorporating nonprint media into the assignment.

LIBRARY RESEARCH PLANS

Level I: Technology

The objectives for this library research plan are as follows:

- The students will be introduced to specific reference materials found in the media center.
- The students will use specific references to complete a quiz about inventions.
- The students will find information about a contemporary invention.
- The students will think creatively about technology and the future.
- The students will communicate their ideas with drawings and words.

Make copies of Figures 8-1 and 8-2, and distribute them to your students. Here are the answers to the quiz:

1. f	6. i
2. g	7. j
3. h	8. e
4. a	9. b
5. k	10. c

Level II: Research Checklist

The objectives for this library research plan are as follows:

- The students will evaluate their research process.
- The students will focus on the weaknesses in their research strategy.
- The students will perceive the research process as a search into varied and diverse sources of information.
- The students will be informed of resources previously overlooked.

Make copies of Figure 8-3 and distribute them to your students.

Level III: Nineteenth-Century Movements

The objectives for this library research plan are as follows:

- The students will use a variety of media center resources to locate information about the principal movements and influential people of the nineteenth century.
- The students will work in groups to focus their research for participation in a panel discussion as a culminating activity.
- The students' research will reinforce skills in locating information through use of subject and author entries in the card catalog.
- The students' research will require the use of standard reference books in literature, art, and music.

- The students will use dictionaries in the fields of social sciences and the arts to become informed about terms applied to the movements of the nineteenth century.

Make copies of Figures 8-4 through 8-6, and distribute them to your students.

Name _____   Class _____

Date _____

ASSIGNMENT FOR TECHNOLOGY

There are three parts to this assignment. Due date: _____

A. Below are ten inventions from the period of the Industrial Revolution. Match the invention in column A with the proper inventor in column B. Write the correct letter from column B on the appropriate line. Be careful!

A	B
_____ 1. cotton gin	a. Samuel Morse
_____ 2. steamboat	b. John Kay
_____ 3. spinning jenny	c. Alexander Graham Bell
_____ 4. telegraph	d. Thomas Edison
_____ 5. airplane	e. George Stephenson
_____ 6. sewing machine	f. Eli Whitney
_____ 7. steam engine	g. Robert Fulton
_____ 8. railroad	h. James Hargreaves
_____ 9. flying shuttle	i. Elias Howe
_____ 10. telephone	j. James Watt
	k. Orville Wright

B. Choose an invention of the 20th century. Research the history of that invention. Write three paragraphs about the invention. The first paragraph should tell when it was invented and by whom. The second paragraph should tell briefly what it was designed to do. In the third paragraph, tell how you think the invention has benefited civilization (or perhaps it has not been a benefit!).

C. Think about the 21st century and a futuristic invention of your own. Make a drawing of your invention and write about it in two paragraphs. The first paragraph should tell what the invention is designed to do and what you will call it. The second paragraph should tell how you think it will benefit mankind.

   THE MEDIA SPECIALIST HAS PREPARED A GUIDE TO HELP YOU COMPLETE THIS ASSIGNMENT.

GUIDE FOR TECHNOLOGY 8–2

A. **Use these references for the first part of the assignment:**

1. *Reader's Encyclopedia* (arranged alphabetically by subject or proper name)

2. Unabridged dictionaries

3. *Who Was Who in America*

4. *Dictionary of American Biography*

5. *Webster's Biographical Dictionary*

6. Master index to an encyclopedia

7. Indexes to books about U.S. history and the history of Great Britain

8. _____

9. _____

These subject headings may be used in the card catalog for additional sources:
GREAT BRITAIN—HISTORY (941.08)
UNITED STATES—HISTORY (973.9)
INVENTORS (or the proper name of the inventor)

B. **Use these subject headings in the card catalog and in magazine indexes for the second part of the assignment:**
INVENTIONS
INVENTORS
TECHNOLOGY
TECHNOLOGY AND CIVILIZATION (or the name of the inventor or the invention you have selected)

C. **Use these subject headings in the card catalog, the magazine indexes, or indexes to the media center's sources of current topics for the third part of the assignment:**
TWENTY-FIRST CENTURY
FUTURE LIFE
TECHNOLOGY
TECHNOLOGY AND CIVILIZATION
ENGINEERING
SCIENCE AND CIVILIZATION

Name _____   Class _____

Date _____

8–3   **RESEARCH CHECKLIST**

    This checklist is designed to help you evaluate the manner in which you conducted your research in the media center. It is unlikely that you will have used all of the sources that are mentioned here.

    After you have completed the checklist, please show it to the media specialist. IT WILL NOT BE GRADED. You may then keep the checklist to help you with your next research assignment.

My topic was: _____

A.   I used the following references to help me narrow down my topic:

    _____ Reading and Study Guide in *World Book Encyclopedia*

    _____ *Readers' Guide to Periodical Literature*

    _____ The *New York Times Index*

    _____ The study guides to SIRS

    _____ The study guides in *Encyclopedia of World Biography*

    _____ *Harvard Guide to American History*

    _____ _____

    _____ _____

B.   I found information in the following types of references:

    _____ Dictionaries   _____ Government manuals

    _____ Encyclopedias   _____ Statistical almanacs

    _____ Atlases   _____ Biographies

    _____ Almanacs   _____ Audiovisual programs

C.   I located my sources and information by:

    _____ Using the card catalog   _____ Asking the librarian

    _____ Browsing   _____ Using indexes in books

    _____ _____

D.   Other sources that were useful for current information were:

    _____ *Current Biography*   _____ *Facts-on-File*

    _____ NewsBank®   _____ Daily newspaper

    _____ *Congressional Quarterly Weekly Reports*   _____ Magazine indexes

    _____ Computer data base   _____ Vertical file

E.   These sources suggested further readings on my topic:

    _____ *Books in Print*   _____ Bibliography in a book

    _____ Bibliography in an encyclopedia   _____ Data base search

    _____ _____

Name _____   Class _____

Date _____

ASSIGNMENT FOR NINETEENTH-CENTURY MOVEMENTS   8–4

In the media center, you will find a variety of materials for your research about the nineteenth-century movements. They will consist of reference books, novels, biographies and autobiographies, audiovisuals, and samples of art, poetry, and essays on these topics:

Romanticism, per se

Romanticism as expressed in literature, music, and art

Realism, per se

Realism as expressed in literature, music, and art

Socialism

Marxism

Nationalism

Liberalism

Darwinism

Domestic system of manufacturing

Factory system of manufacturing

A list of authors, artists, and musicians from this period is attached to this assignment. As you research the lives of these persons, look for samples of their work.

You will have _____ class periods to conduct preliminary research in these materials, using them in the media center.

After that time, on _____, we will organize ourselves into groups for research into specific topics and panel presentations on those topics.

Start this assignment by reading the guide your media specialist has prepared.

8–5   GUIDE FOR NINETEENTH-CENTURY MOVEMENTS

Review these research strategies for this assignment:

1. To locate works *by* a person on your list, use the author entry to the card catalog (last name first).

2. To locate information *about* an individual, use the subject entry to the card catalog (last name first).

3. To locate general information about the arts, use a subject heading such as:
   MUSIC—DICTIONARIES
   MUSIC—HISTORY AND CRITICISM
   ENCYCLOPEDIAS AND DICTIONARIES

4. To locate information about social movements, use such subject headings as:
   SOCIAL MOVEMENTS
   HISTORY, MODERN 1800–1899 (19th century)
   POLITICAL SCIENCE—DICTIONARIES
   SOCIALISM

5. Do not neglect to follow up on ''See'' and ''See also'' references.

6. Subject entries should lead you to reference books as well as materials in the general collection and the vertical files.

7. Audiovisual materials should be helpful and are located by subject entries.

8. Large picture books, marked ''oversize'' on the catalog cards, will provide examples of artists' works.

9. The *Readers' Guide to Periodical Literature* will help you locate comprehensive historical articles.

10. Other resources that should not be overlooked are:

_____

_____

Name _____ Class _____

Date _____

NINETEENTH-CENTURY
AUTHORS, ARTISTS, AND MUSICIANS
8–6

AUTHORS	ARTISTS	MUSICIANS
William Blacke	John Constable	Ludwig van Beethoven
Sir Walter Scott	J. M. W. Turner	Felix Mendelssohn
Samuel Coleridge	Ferdinand Delacroix	Frederic Chopin
William Wordsworth	Jean Corot	Richard Wagner
Lord Byron	Francisco Goya	Giuseppe Verdi
John Keats	Jean Millet	Johannes Brahms
Victor Hugo	Gustave Courbet	A. Claude Debussy
Alexandre Dumas (père)	Honoré Daumier	
Johann von Goethe	Winslow Homer	
Washington Irving	James Whistler	
Nathaniel Hawthorne	Sarah Newmeyer	
Edgar Allan Poe	Claude Monet	
Ralph Waldo Emerson	Edouard Manet	
Walt Whitman	Camille Pissaro	
Percy Shelley	Pierre Renoir	
Charles Dickens	Edgar Degas	
Honoré de Balzac	Toulouse Lautrec	
Gustave Flaubert	Paul Cézanne	
Émile Zola	Eugene Gauguin	
Samuel Clemens	Vincent van Gogh	
Nikolai Gogol		
Fyodor Dostoyevsky		
Ivan Turgenev		
Auguste Comte		
Herbert Spencer		

APRIL BULLETIN BOARDS

April Fool's Day
Pan American Day
International Children's Book Week
World Health Day
Secretaries' Day
National Arbor Day
Library Week
Keep America Beautiful Week

A Nation of Immigrants

An interesting bulletin board can be created for April using the theme: A NATION OF IMMIGRANTS. Since it involves selections from autobiographies or biographies of foreign-born Americans, it can stimulate reading.

Place your caption at the top of the board and then center a map of the world. A world map from your vertical file or from a back issue of *National Geographic* may be used for the period of time that the display is up. If you are interested in a small-sized map, you may borrow one from a back-file of *Facts-On-File*. An outline of a world map can be made using the techniques described earlier for enlarging illustrations with an overhead or opaque projector.

Select the biographical titles you want to highlight. Make photocopies of the title pages and make them into posters by mounting them on construction paper. If a picture is available of the person, add it to the poster.

Arrange your posters strategically around the world map and link the poster to the country which is the birthplace of the individual. This connection can be made with yarn of varying colors which will show up against the background of the map.

You will need only these materials for this display:

• Construction paper

• Yarn

• Map of the world

• Title pages from selected biographies.

INSERVICE AND PUBLIC RELATIONS:
FORMING POLICIES REGARDING COPYRIGHT RESTRICTIONS

Media specialists in the schools have an ethical and legal responsibility to become informed regarding the Copyrights Act of 1976 and the guidelines which have been developed since the passage of the legislation regarding the applicability of the "fair use" doctrine of the law. We deal on a daily basis with the provisions of the law and are obligated to observe the restrictions, as well as to inform those persons using our services about the law.

The administrators and the school board should develop policies for compliance with the copyright laws and expect staff and teachers to follow them. Too often such policies are not in place and, as new technologies are adopted, indiviuals are left to follow their own discretion in compliance with the copyright provisions. Regrettably, noncompliance is often the result, as teachers bend the rules with the mistaken belief that "fair use" for educators means freedom to copy at will.

Since we are the professionals providing many of the materials that are so desirable for classroom use, as well as the equipment that makes copying those materials so easy, we must inform ourselves regarding the copyright regulations and take steps to inform teachers.

It is important to note that penalties for infringement of copyright can be substantial. Educators risk damage to their professional reputations as well. The temptation to reproduce copyrighted materials is overwhelming, given the gap that too often exists between educational dollars and the costs of commercially prepared materials. Nevertheless, a commitment to protection of copyright by living within the interpretation of fair use must be made by media specialists and teachers alike.

As first steps toward realizing this commitment, the school media specialist should:

1. Become familiar with the law and the guidelines for its interpretation. Publications regarding the law are available from the copyright office of the Library of Congress.

2. Present the basic tenets of the law to the faculty at a faculty meeting or in a newsletter. Audiovisual programs are available from the Association for Educational Communications and Technology (1126 16th Street, N.W., Washington, D.C. 20036) for just such inservice purposes.

3. Make your philosophical commitment to compliance known to all who use your services.

4. Post copyright warning notices near your photocopier and on a bulletin board near the audiovisual work station.

Gary Becker, author of *The Copyright Game Resource Guide* (available from Mr. Becker, 1770 Blackmon Court, Longwood, Florida 32779), grants, with purchase of the resource, permission to reproduce sections of the guide as well as the many forms he includes.

The following transparency masters may be helpful to you until you can obtain other aids or produce your own. As with any overhead transparencies you use in a presentation, these are intended as cues for your remarks.

FAIR USE

Educators' Copyright Guidelines

"Fair Use"* is intended:

1) To protect authors' and artists' work

2) To allow for infor- mational needs of educators

*Section 107-1976 Copyright Act

PHOTOCOPYING

Single copies usually o.k.

Multiple copies IF
   Brief, spontaneous,
   not repeated

NEVER for producing one's own
   anthology OR to substitute
   for purchase

AUDIOVISUAL MATERIALS

Must be:
   Legal copy with copyright notice
   included

   Used as part of instructional program
      -In classroom or school
      -Only to students and educators

OFF-AIR VIDEOTAPING

-At request of teacher

-Shown to students twice in 10-day period

-Viewed for evaluation for 45 days

-Must include copyright notice

RECOMMENDATIONS

-Read fuller explanation of guidelines

-Request legal permission from publishers

-Suggest purchase of materials

OUR GOAL IS TO
PROVIDE QUALITY
MATERIALS THAT
HAVE BEEN
ACQUIRED LEGALLY
AND CAN BE
USED CONFIDENTLY.

Respect the law
and model that
respect for
students!

May

*"Rough winds do shake the darling buds of May,
And summer's lease hath all too short a date."*

William Shakespeare
Sonnets XVIII

May Birthdays

1688	Alexander Pope
1803	Ralph Waldo Emerson
1812	Robert Browning
1812	Edward Lear
1819	Walt Whitman
1859	Arthur Conan Doyle
1882	Sigrid Undset
1892	Archibald MacLeish
1903	Scott O'Dell
1907	Irene Hunt
1907	Daphne du Maurier
1908	Ian Fleming
1912	John Cheever
1912	May Sarton
1921	Farley Mowat
1923	Joseph Heller
1925	Harry Mazer
1925	Tony Hellerman
1926	Peter Shaffer
1927	Robert Ludlum
1930	Lorraine Hansberry
1930	John Barth
1931	Norma Fox Mazer
1936	Paul Zindel
1937	Roger Zelazny
1938	Norma Klein
1947	Corinne Bliss

MANAGEMENT TASKS

"Sir, as your mandate did request,
I send you here a faithfu' list . . ."

Robert Burns
The Inventory

Your management tasks for the month of May are:

1. Taking inventory
2. Weeding and withdrawing materials

Taking Inventory

Taking inventory of the media center collection seems to have been, historically, the burden media specialists worried about all school year, then stoically—no…complaining all the way—raised to their shoulders during the last few days of school. Some, citing the importance of accounting for materials, have managed to negotiate days just before the year's end when the center can be closed and time can be devoted to inventory procedures. Ideally, it is a tidy and satisfying process, this accounting, when one can retrieve materials, shelve and read shelves, and then proceed to inventory.

Even under these circumstances, however, this particular task tends to be done hastily. Often, as a result of inadequate staffing, it requires locating volunteers, spending training time with them, and ending the year on a negative note. It is far better to spend those last days of the school year assisting students with their unfinished reports, reflecting upon the years's successes and failures, composing a meaningful summary of activities for one's principal, making plans for the coming year, accomplishing some satisfying organization of records and files, and perhaps hosting a farewell tea for the departing class, your staff, or the school staff.

I am sure my bias is showing. Somehow, the inventory does not assume for me the great importance I find that it does for many school media specialists. There seems to be little reason the inventory cannot be a continuous process realized during the last half of the school year. It can then be done in small, manageable sections, using procedures outlined later in this chapter. Whether the inventory tasks are assigned to support staff or to volunteers, they require a healthy portion of professional involvement, developing the procedures and supervising their completion, and deciding which materials to withdraw, discard or repair.

Schedule the inventory by classification and type of media. Start with the materials which circulate least; plan to inventory reference books last.

1. Materials should be arranged on the shelf in the same order as the cards appear in the shelf list.
2. Match the accession number of the materials to the number on the shelf list card:
   a. If the shelf list and item agree, write the year at the top right-hand corner of the circulation card.
   b. If there is a discrepancy, place the shelf list card in the item and set aside for resolution.

3. If the item is missing, put a paper clip on the shelf list card. If more than one copy is listed on the shelf list card, write "M" followed by the year near the accession number on the card.

4. If an item that was previously missing is on the shelf, erase the "missing" date on the shelf list card, remove the paper clips from the card, and write the inventory year date on the right-hand corner of the circulation card.

5. As a drawer of cards is inventoried, check the cards with clips against the circulation at the desk. If an item is in circulation, remove the clip from the shelf list card and mark the circulation card with the date.

6. Materials that are badly worn or damaged should be removed from the shelf and the shelf list card placed with them, as they are candidates for withdrawal.

7. When a card has accumulated three clips (or whatever number you decide upon), the title should be considered lost and you should proceed to pull all cards or to replace the material.

This is a simple, but time-consuming procedure for taking inventory. It is effective since one can count losses simply by counting clips. And, there are benefits to handling each and every book. One can then make the best decisions about weeding and about the status of the total collection. However, as you look ahead to automation in your media center, plan carefully to make the inventory procedures a part of the system. If you enter your collection into a computer program, plan at the same time to bar-code each item. Code scanners then make it possible to inventory as a continuous process as items circulate. Your program will keep your inventory statistics for you. Hand-held cordless scanners are available which allow you to inventory at the shelves, eliminating even the transporting of the non-circulating items to the computer. With such a device, you simply pull the item off the shelf, pass the "wand" over the bar code, and slip the item back in place. When you have reached the capacity of the scanner, download the information into your computer and continue with your inventory.

Your computer program should be capable of accepting the accession codes, tallying the numbers, counting the numbers, counting the number of missing codes, and printing out the titles of the missing items. Most book jobbers will offer the service of attaching the bar codes to your books before shipment.

It has been my experience that utilizing volunteers in the media center is less than satisfactory. There are two major drawbacks:

1. Volunteers are just that, volunteers. Other commitments often interfere with their schedules; and

2. Having a coterie of volunteers in the media center may be counter-productive to your goal of acquiring paid support staff.

However, the use of volunteer time is most productive when volunteers are recruited for a specific task. If you plan your inventory for an intense, limited period of time, you may want to consider a volunteer team for the task.

There are several ways you can locate volunteers:

1. Ask your principal to publicize your need in his or her communications to parents.

2. Attend parent-faculty meetings and make a personal appeal for help.

3. Write a news release for district or town papers, stating your specific need and exactly what days and hours you can use the assistance.

4. Ask for student volunteers through the school bulletin.

Weeding and Withdrawing Materials

You are now, during this month, involved in the professional responsibility of taking stock of your collection and continuing your selection of materials. Concomitant to this responsibility is the task of selecting the materials which should be removed from the collection. There are a number of reasons "weeding" is important. Curriculum requirements may have changed and rendered material useless; you may have a problem with space; materials may be outdated or biased; or items may have become damaged and lost their appeal.

There are model policies for weeding to be found in library literature. Generally, you want to make your decisions about withdrawal of material based on its accuracy and relevancy to the curriculum, its historical value, its physical condition, and whether it is dispensable. You will want to refrain from discarding titles which were gifts to the school, have local significance, or in some respect, meet the description of a classic in literature.

Having decided to remove a title from the collection, follow this procedure:

1. Mark "withdrawn" by the accession number on the shelf list, and add the year.

2. If all accession numbers are marked on a shelf list card in this way, the shelf list card and cards in the public catalog should be pulled.

3. Keep these cards in a "withdrawn" file. You may replace the titles. You will want the numbers to update your inventory.

4. Remove the pockets and circulation cards from the materials.

5. Stamp "withdrawn" across all property markings in the material.

6. Withdrawn materials should be destroyed unless they can be donated to another institution. If given to students or teachers, they will come back to haunt you.

7. Remove titles from bibliographies you have on file.

8. Video and audio tapes may be erased and reused.

The H.W. Wilson catalogs of standard collections for school media collections are excellent sources for helping you determine the value of a title.

If you have an automated system of circulation control you can compute the use of any given title and, by storing the acquisition dates as well as establishing a shelf-life period for materials, you can factor in the time to consider weeding.

LIBRARY RESEARCH PLANS

Level I: *The Odyssey*

The following are the objectives for this library research plan:

• The students will extrapolate a situation from classical literature to modern times.

• The students will locate Greek myths in the media center collections.

- The students will recite orally in class.
- The students will communicate ideas in play form.
- The students will locate and use musical resources in the media center.
- The students will gain skill in writing a storyboard.
- The students will communicate their ideas about *The Odyssey* in visual forms.
- The students will use a video camera and recorder.

Make copies of Figures 9-1 and 9-2 and distribute them to your students.

Level II: Modern American Poetry

The objectives for this library research plan are as follows:

- The students will use reserve materials in the media center.
- The students will use poetry indexes, the card catalog, and magazine indexes to locate poems, literary criticism, and biographical information.
- The students will read poetry and interpret its themes.
- The students will relate the life experiences of a poet to the poet's work.
- The students will answer specific questions about the poet and his or her work.
- The students will communicate their thoughts about the questions in written form.

Make copies of Figures 9-3 and 9-4, and distribute them to your students.

Level III: Poetry Quotations

The objectives of this library research plan are as follows:

- The students will use dictionaries of literary quotations.
- The students will read poetry for meaning and be able to paraphrase.
- The students will use biographical sources to learn about a poet's life and work.
- The students will use periodical indexes and current news sources to find articles about a poet and his or her work.
- The students will use the card catalog and bibliographies to locate material about a poet.
- The students will use books of literary criticism to learn about forms of poetry.
- The students will express their understanding of a poet's work by reciting a selection from it or by written analysis.
- The students will use proper bibliographic form in the writing assignment.

Make copies of Figures 9-5 and 9-6 and distribute them to your students. Here is the key to the quotations:

1. Robert Frost. *The Death of the Hired Man*
2. Robert Frost. *Birches*
3. William Wordsworth. *Hart-Leap Well*
4. William Wordsworth. *I Wandered Lonely As a Cloud*

5. Percy Bysshe Shelley. *Adonais*
6. John Keats. *Ode on a Grecian Urn*
7. John Keats. *Ode to a Nightingale*
8. Samuel Taylor Coleridge. *The Ancient Mariner*
9. Lord George Byron. *She Walks in Beauty*
10. William Blake. *The Lamb*
11. Elizabeth Barrett Browning. *Andrea del Sarto*
12. Robert Browning. *My Last Duchess*
13. Elizabeth Barrett Browning. *Sonnets from the Portuguese*
14. Robert Burns. *My Love Is Like a Red Red Rose*
15. Robert Burns. *To a Mouse*
16. Robert Burns. *To a Louse*
17. Robert Burns. *Coming Through the Rye*
18. William Blake. *The Tyger*
19. John Keats. *La Belle Dame Sans Merci*
20. Percy Bysshe Shelley. *Ozymandias*
21. Percy Bysshe Shelley. *Adonais*
22. Walt Whitman. *Give Me the Splendid Silent Sun*
23. Emily Dickinson. *Because I Could Not Stop for Death*
24. Emily Dickinson. *I Heard a Fly Buzz When I Died*
25. Emily Dickinson. *What Soft-Cherubic Creatures*
26. e. e. cummings. *& (AND)*
27. Percy Bysshe Shelley. *Ode to the West Wind*
28. Alfred Lord Tennyson. *Crossing the Bar*
29. Rudyard Kipling. *The White Man's Burden*
30. John Lennon and Paul McCartney. *Yesterday*
31. T. S. Eliot. *The Hollow Men*
32. Helen Reddy. *I Am Woman*
33. Rudyard Kipling. *If*
34. Rudyard Kipling. *The Ballad of East and West*
35. Alfred Lord Tennyson. *Charge of the Light Brigade*
36. William Shakespeare. *Twelfth Night*
37. William Shakespeare. *Tempest*
38. Robert Frost. *Stopping by Woods on a Snowy Evening*
39. T. S. Eliot. *The Love Song of J. Alfred Prufrock*
40. John Keats. *Lines Supposed to Have Been Addressed to Fanny Browne*
41. Ogden Nash. *Reflections on Ice-Breaking*
42. A. A. Milne. *When We Were Very Young*

43. Robert Frost. *Fire and Ice*
44. A. A. Milne. *Vespers*
45. A. A. Milne. *Disobedience*
46. Dante. *The Divine Comedy*
47. Robert Frost. *North of Boston; Mending Wall*
48. Rudyard Kipling. *Gunga Din*
49. Edgar Allan Poe. *The Raven*
50. William Shakespeare. *As You Like It*
51. Henry W. Longfellow. *The Arrow and the Song*
52. Henry W. Longfellow. *The Village Blacksmith*
53. Clement Clark Moore. *A Visit from St. Nicholas*
54. Alfred Lord Tennyson. *The Charge of the Light Brigade*
55. William Wordsworth. *The World Is too Much with Us*
56. Ogden Nash. *Free Wheeling; The Baby*
57. William Shakespeare. *A Mid-Summer Night's Dream*
58. Lewis Carroll. *Through the Looking Glass*
59. Edgar Lee Masters. *Spoon River Anthology; Ann Rutledge*
60. Langston Hughes. *Harlem*
61. Carl Sandburg. *Fog*
62. Edna St. Vincent Millay. *A Few Figs from Thistles; First Fig*
63. Dame Edith Sitwell. *Still Falls the Rain*
64. Ogden Nash. *Song of the Open Road*
65. Dylan Thomas. *Do Not Go Gentle into That Good Night*
66. Gwendolyn Brooks. *Beckonings; Boys; Black*
67. W. B. Yeats. *The Second Coming*
68. Lewis Carroll. *Alice's Adventures in Wonderland*
69. Lewis Carroll. *Alice's Adventures in Wonderland*
70. Ben Jonson. *Song to Celia*
71. Keith Richards and Mick Jagger. *Sympathy for the Devil*
72. John Milton. *On His Blindness*
73. Andrew Marvell. *To His Coy Mistress*
74. Bob Dylan. *Blowin' in the Wind*
75. Walt Whitman. *Leaves of Grass; Song of Myself*

Name _____   Class _____

Date _____

GUIDE FOR *THE ODYSSEY*

1. To locate Greek myths in the media center collection, use the following subject headings in the card catalog:

   MYTHOLOGY, CLASSICAL

   LEGENDS—GREEK

   Some of the titles will be found in the regular collection; others will be reference materials. Audiovisual materials, such as records and audiotapes, will be found by using the card catalog.

2. You may use audiovisual equipment by _____

   _____

   _____

3. The media specialist has a sample storyboard for your use.

4. Ideas for your artwork may be found among oversized picture books:

   MYTHOLOGY (200's)

   ART (700's)

5. You may practice your oral presentation in this area: _____

   _____

6. Ask the media specialist for paper, markers, and other supplies needed for your artwork.

Name _____   Class _____

Date _____

PROJECT IDEAS FOR *THE ODYSSEY*   9–2

A description of your project, for preliminary approval, is due:

_____

The final project is due: _____

1. Write a modern-day version of an episode from *The Odyssey*. Submit a written version, but be prepared to perform this version orally, as the bards did.

2. Research and learn a Greek myth and then present it orally using music, gestures, etc., as a bard or storyteller would. Submit the myth written out in your own words, in a paraphrase of the original.

3. Act out an episode from *The Odyssey*. Submit a script with stage directions and include music suitable for the episode.

4. Write and present a 60-second television commercial for a real or invented product of the 1980's using characters and situations from *The Odyssey*. A script and a storyboard are required.

5. Take an episode from *The Odyssey* and pretend you are a television reporter doing a live telecast. Schedule use of the video equipment for taping and present the videotape to the class. A storyboard is required.

6. Choose an episode from *The Odyssey* and report upon it. Illustrate your report with photos, famous art, album covers, ads, or posters.

Name _____   Class _____

Date _____

ASSIGNMENT FOR MODERN AMERICAN POETRY   9–3

Assignment: Choose one poet from the list provided. Then read at least 12 of his or her poems, background material on the poet's life, influences on the poet's life, and literary criticism of the poet's work.

Material is on reserve in the media center. Additionally, be sure to use these resources:

- Card catalog (subject entries are your poet's name and AMERICAN POETRY—HISTORY AND CRITICISM and AMERICAN LITERATURE—HISTORY AND CRITICISM)
- Poetry indexes
- *Readers' Guide to Periodical Literature*

- _____

- _____

Your research paper should contain the following information:

1. A brief account of the poet's life, significant events and influences

2. Analyses of at least four of the poet's works

Your paper should answer these questions:

1. What facts about the poet's life are of interest in the appreciation of his or her poetry?

2. What are the principal recurring themes in the poetry? (Love, nature, death, search for meaning, commentary on man and society, etc., are possible themes.)

3. What kinds of people does your poet write about? How does he or she feel about people?

4. What images, symbols, similes, metaphors, or personifications does your poet use?

5. What special sound effects (alliteration, rhyme) does he or she use?

6. What do you consider to be the chief qualities of your poet?

7. Which poem did you enjoy most? Why? Describe how it affected you.

Your analyses should include illustrations of the points you want to make.

Your paper is due: _____

Name _____   Class _____

Date _____

9–4   **MODERN AMERICAN POETS**

Robert Frost	Langston Hughes
Vachel Lindsay	Edgar Lee Masters
Stephen Vincent Benét	Elinor Wylie
Alan Seeger	Sara Teasdale
Carl Sandburg	James Weldon Johnson
e. e. cummings	Edna St. Vincent Millay
Archibald MacLeish	W. H. Auden
Theodore Roethke	Mark Van Doren
Richard Eberhart	Karl Shapiro
Ogden Nash	Richard Wilbur
Walt Whitman	Richard Armour
Emily Dickinson	Sidney Lanier
Stephen Crane	Edwin Arlington Robinson
James Whitcomb Riley	Edwin Markham
Robinson Jeffers	Lawrence Ferlinghetti
William Carlos Williams	Amy Lowell
Marianne Moore	Ezra Pound
John Ciardi	Wallace Stevens
Shel Silverstein	Randall Jarrell
Robert Penn Warren	Countee Cullen
Denise Levertov	John Greenleaf Whittier
Paul Lawrence Dunbar	Hart Crane
Robert Lowell	Allen Ginsberg
John Crowe Ransom	Ralph Waldo Emerson

Name _____ Class _____

Date _____

9–5   POETRY ASSIGNMENT

1. Choose a quotation from the list provided. Find the poem from which your quotation originates. These reference books are a good place to start:

   Oxford Dictionary of Quotations

   Bartlett's Familiar Quotations

   _____

2. Your quote is relatively famous, so do not give up. Give the source in which you found the quote. Use acceptable footnote form.

3. Using these sources, find the poem. Copy it and underline your quote.

   Granger's Index to Poetry

   _____

   _____

   The card catalog

4. Paraphrase your poem. Your translation might be shorter than the original, but usually it will be much longer. State your poem's general meaning.

5. Write a two-page biography of your poet. Give all important dates, titles of major works, and any interesting details you find. Give at least four sources for your information.

   The card catalog (using your poet's name as a subject entry)

   The Reader's Encyclopedia

   _____

   _____

6. Do a full etymology, including earliest usage, of three words longer than five letters in your poem. Give the word's poetic function. For example, is it part of a metaphor, image, personification, etc.? Tell the source of your information in acceptable footnote form. These sources will be helpful:

   The Oxford Dictionary of the English Language

   Dictionary of Literary Terms

7. Give the titles of ten books or magazine articles about your poet, the poem, or the poet's style or era. Write the titles in acceptable bibliographic form.

> The card catalog
> *The Readers' Guide to Periodical Literature*
> *Books in Print*

> _____

8. Write a poem similar to the one you studied. This means similar in topic, structure, use of poetic devices, etc.

9. Prepare to recite in class the poem you studied and the poem you wrote.

The written portions of this assignment are due: _____

Oral presentations will start: _____

9–6   **QUOTATIONS**

1. Home is the place where, when you have to go there, they have to take you in.

2. I'd like to get away from earth awhile.

3. The moving accident is not my trade.

4. I wandered lonely as a cloud.

5. I weep for Adonais—he is dead!

6. Beauty is truth, truth beauty

7. My heart aches, and a drowsy numbness pain

8. Water, water, every where/Nor any drop to drink

9. She walks in beauty, like the night

10. Little lamb, who made thee?/Dost thou know who made thee?

11. Ah, but a man's reach should exceed his grasp/Or what's a heaven for?

12. That's my last Duchess painted on the wall/Looking as if she were alive

13. How do I love thee?/Let me count the ways

14. O' my luve's like a red red rose/That's newly sprung in June

15. The best laid schemes o' mice an' men

16. O wad some Pow'r the giftie gie us/To see oursels as others see us!

17. Coming through the Rye

18. What immortal hand or eye/Could frame thy fearful symmetry?

19. I see a lily on thy brow

20. I met a traveler from an Antique land

21. He hath awakened from the dream of life

22. Give me the splendid silent sun with all his beams full-dazzling!

23. The Carriage held but just Ourselves/And Immortality

24. I heard a Fly buzz—when I died.

25. What soft cherubic creatures/These gentlewomen are

26. Who knows if the moon's/A balloon, coming out of a keen city

27. O wild west wind, thou breath of Autumn's being

28. And may there be no moaning of the bar/When I put out to sea

29. Take up the white man's burden

30. There's a shadow hanging over me

31. We are the Hollow men/We are the stuffed men

32. If I have to, I can do anything

33. If you can keep your head when all about you men are losing theirs

34. Oh, East is East, and West is West

35. Half a league, half a league/Half a league onward

36. If music be the food of love, play on

37. We are such stuff/As dreams are made of

38. The woods are lovely, dark and deep

39. I have measured out my life with coffee spoons

40. This living hand, now warm and capable

41. Candy is dandy

42. They're changing guard at Buckingham Palace

43. Some say the world will end in Fire

44. Hush! Hush! Whisper who dares!

45. James James/Morrison Morrison/Weatherby George Dupree

46. All hope abandon, you who enter here

47. Good fences make good neighbors

48. You're a better man than I am/Gunga Din

49. Quoth the raven, ''Nevermore''

50. All the world's a stage

51. I shot an arrow into the air

52. Under the spreading chestnut tree

53. Happy Christmas to all, and to all a good night!

54. Cannon to the right of them, cannon to the left of them

55. The world is too much with us

56. A bit of talcum/Is always walcum

57. Since once I sat upon a promontory/And heard a mermaid on a dolphin's back

58. The walrus and the carpenter/Were walking hand in hand

59. Out of me unworthy and unknown/The vibrations of deathless music

60. What happens to a dream deferred?

61. The fog comes/On little cat feet

62. My candle burns at both ends/It will not last the night

63. Still falls the rain/Dark as the world of man, black as our loss

64. I think that I shall never see/A bill board lovely as a tree

9–6 cont'd.

65. Do not go gentle into that good night

66. Beware the easy griefs/That fool and fuel nothing

67. Turning and turning in the widening gyre/The falcon cannot hear the falconer

68. Twas Brillig, and the slithy toves

69. "You are old, Father William," the young man said

70. Drink to me only with thine eyes

71. Please allow me to introduce myself/I'm a man of wealth and taste

72. They also serve who only stand and wait

73. Had we but world enough, and time/This coyness, Lady, were no crime

74. How many roads must a man walk down

75. I celebrate myself, and sing myself

MAY BULLETIN BOARDS

Law Day
Memorial Day
Mothers' Day
Armed Forces Day
May Day
Peace Day
Indian Day
Loyalty Day
World Red Cross Day
V-E Day
''Freedom to Read'' Anniversary

Poetry for Spring

May seems the perfect month to promote poetry. The world itself is a poem at this time of year. Attract attention to your theme with this thought-provoking quotation from Wallace Stevens: ''A poem is a meteor. . .'' (Be sure to include that credit.)

To complete this bulletin board, you will need:

- Large pieces of dark blue construction paper
- Letters of white construction paper for the caption
- Aluminum foil for stars, or precut stars
- Poetry selections of your choosing

Cover your bulletin board with a deep blue construction paper. Onto this background make a galaxy of silvery stars. Stars of many sizes should be used. These can be purchased commercially, or you can cut them from aluminum foil.

Select short poems and reproduce them for your bulletin board either with large type on a typewriter, or on your computer, or simply print them up with a felt-tip marker. Choose poems that illustrate various forms and express different themes. Limit your selection to just a few at a time, and change the selection that you include on the board. The poems can be stapled in the ''universe'' you created.

INSERVICE AND PUBLIC RELATIONS: PROMOTING READING

As library/media specialists, and dedicated readers ourselves, we may subscribe wholeheartedly to Joseph Addison's observation in *The Tatler* that ''Reading is to the mind what exercise is to the body.'' We know that to promote the art of reading is to promote our services and program. Library literature is replete with strategies for encouraging reading among students and staff in a secondary school. The ideas range from read-ins and read-a-thons to intramural contests and lunch period book talks. You can adapt any number of plans to your particular school setting; most can be reasonably successful, if you have the cooperation of the teachers who can promote the idea in class and contribute their time and talent, as well.

If faculty and students are going to come into your media center to read, and if they are going to check out books from the collection for leisure reading, several conditions must prevail:

. . . You must have a selection of books that meet their interests

. . . They must know the books that are available

. . . The books must be attractive

. . . They must have time to read

. . . The atmosphere in the media center must be conducive to reading

. . . There must be a motivation to read

We can and do affect these conditions. We can see readily how our selection procedures need to accommodate student and teacher input. We know the importance of publicizing our collection through bibliographies and displays. We select attractive titles, and include paperbacks even though many of us would prefer a hardback collection only. We continuously work to promote our centers as quiet study areas, with comfortable leisure-reading seating included.

"Time" and "motivation" are the difficult factors to influence. In most secondary schools today, students are scheduled tightly, and graduation requirements leave little time for pursuing leisure reading interests. Insisting that students use their time wisely and efficiently will help. Making the media center an attractive place to spend free time, rather than in a lounge or smoking area, is a step toward promoting reading as a leisure-time activity.

A powerful motivation to read for many students is an assignment and the subsequent grade. We can cooperate with teachers in reading assignments that include titles which are exciting to their students, and then suggest new ways to report and evaluate that reading. The list of "Twelve Alternatives to the Ho-Hum Book Report" which follows, require our involvement and the use of our facility. They can be effective in livening up the book report and encouraging more reading.

1. Write a "diary" for the main character.
2. *Be* the author. Appear on videotape as the guest of a talk-show host.
3. Select illustrations for the story from the oversized book collection. Copy them with camera and copystand; show the slides as you report on the book.
4. Record your report on audiotape.
5. Dress as a character from the book. Tell the story as a personal experience.
6. Select music to accompany your report.
7. Design a book jacket. Include the review on the inside.
8. If the book is historical, make a timeline of the events.
9. Select one chapter and write the script for a movie or soap opera version.
10. Prepare a storyboard for a television promotion about the book.
11. Act out a scene from the book. Recruit other characters if necessary.
12. Create original illustrations for the book.

Finally, never be afraid to "model" reading. It is totally appropriate for students to see you—the library media specialist—reading a good book!

June

"Keep-deep in June"

Alfred Austin
A Wild Rose

June Birthdays

1572	Ben Jonson
1623	Blaise Pascal
1811	Harriet Beecher Stowe
1840	Thomas Hardy
1842	Ambrose Bierce
1856	Henry Rider Haggard
1865	William Butler Yeats
1875	Thomas Mann
1878	John Masefield
1880	Helen Keller
1892	Pearl S. Buck
1894	Mark Van Doren
1900	Antoine de St. Exupery
1903	George Orwell
1907	Lillian Hellman
1909	Betty Cavanna
1912	Mary McCarthy
1914	John Hersey
1915	Saul Bellow
1925	William Styron
1926	Allen Ginsberg
1933	Jerzy Kosinski
1934	Doris Smith
1938	Joyce Carol Oates
1939	Margaret Drabble
1948	Laurence Yep

MANAGEMENT TASKS

"How forcible are right words!"

Job 6:25

It is time to wrap things up! Your tasks for this final month of the school year are:

1. Preparing your annual report
2. Preparing for closing

Preparing Your Annual Report

It may not have occurred to your principal to request a report from you that summarizes your program. If this is the case, the temptation will be to be relieved and not to prepare one. There are many tasks to complete before you can feel good about closing for the summer, and one less requirement would be welcome.

However, such a report serves more than one purpose. Just as you took time from a very busy schedule at the beginning of the year to plan and look ahead, you need, at this time, to reflect and take time to evaluate your progress. To do so is a way of looking ahead to the next year. As Galsworthy wrote, "if we do not think about the future, we cannot have one."

Whether it is requested or not, your principal will be gratified to receive a summary from you. It will add to his or her awareness of your program. The summary is a vehicle for expressing appreciation for support and for outlining those needs which, if filled, will move your program ahead in the future.

Your report need not be extensive. In fact, the principal will appreciate brevity. It should, however, include these sections:

1. *Budget.* Compare the total funds allocated to your media program over the past three years. Include any special funds or grants received.

2. *Acquisitions.* Include total items acquired in several categories such as books, audio-visual programs, periodicals, etc. Your accession numbers are the source for this information. Again, use a three-year comparison, if possible.

3. *Total collection.* Your administrator can use these figures time after time. Include figures for print and nonprint materials.

4. *Inventory.* Report your losses and numbers of items withdrawn. A comparison with former years is meaningful.

5. *Media center use.* How many classes did your staff serve? Was your center scheduled for other purposes?

6. *Professional activities.* Include professional activities that your staff engaged in during the year. Professional association memberships are appropriate, also.

7. *Looking ahead.* Suggest here the areas where you felt staff and student needs were unmet. What aspects of a good media program were unfulfilled due to need?

186

Preparing for Closing

Once you have completed the report to your administrator, you can devote attention to preparing your media center for summer closing.

If you and your staff can complete the tasks I am listing here before the end of the school year, your opening in the fall should be accomplished quite smoothly. If you established the log I suggested at the beginning of the year, this is now the time to read it over. What you are interested in doing is avoiding the problems you encountered during the past year.

1. Label a section at the circulation desk for summer loan.
2. Inventory your forms and send out masters for duplication over the summer.
3. Prepare work orders for maintenance which will have to be done during the summer.
4. Prepare equipment to be sent out for repair.
5. Pack and label books for the bindery.
6. Complete as many purchase orders as possible.
7. Set up your budget book for the coming year.
8. Label large boxes for collection of summer mail.
9. Do some housecleaning of files, particularly outdated catalogs.
10. Cover equipment and secure it.
11. Finally, try to enjoy the last few days. If possible, keep your schedule open.

LIBRARY RESEARCH PLANS

Level I: Applied Biology

The following are the objectives for this library research plan:

- The students will research a specific animal disease using media center resources.
- The students will use an unabridged dictionary, general encyclopedias, and references about animals.
- The students will complete a worksheet which reflects the results of their research.
- The students will cite the sources of their information.

Make copies of Figures 10-1 and 10-2, and distribute them to your students.

Level II: Foreign Foods

The objectives for this library research plan are as follows:

- The students will locate information about a specific country and its social life and customs.
- The students will use atlases and prepare a map of the country chosen.
- The students will learn about the culture of a country by finding information about its foods and their preparation.
- The students will prepare a foreign food and share it with the class.

- The students will cite the sources they used in correct bibliographic form.
- The students will write a brief report about the country chosen.

Make copies of Figures 10-3 and 10-4, and distribute them to your students.

Level III: Visiting Another Library

The objectives for this library research plan are as follows:

- The students will use locational skills in a library setting that differs from the home school.
- The students will use research strategies to complete a skills exercise.
- The students will observe differences in classification schemes, housing and circulation of materials, and methods of accessing information.

Make copies of Figures 10-5 and 10-6 and distribute them to your students.

GUIDE TO APPLIED BIOLOGY

The following are the references you will use for this assignment:

1. Unabridged dictionaries. These are located _____
   _____

2. General encyclopedias. These sets are located _____
   _____

3. Special references about animals:

   _____
   _____
   _____
   _____

   These are located _____
   _____

Name _____ Class _____

Date _____

APPLIED BIOLOGY WORKSHEET

Using references in the media center, answer as many of these questions as you can. The media specialist has prepared a guide to help you.

Name of the disease to be researched: _____

    1. What causes this disease in animals? _____

    2. What animals get this disease? _____

       Is it a zoonosis? _____

    3. What are the symptoms? _____

    _____

    4. Look up *vector* in an unabridged dictionary. Does this disease have a vector? _____

    5. How can the disease be controlled or prevented? _____

    _____

    6. Can it be cured? _____ If so, how? _____

    _____

    7. Is the cure practical for wild animals or only for domestic ones? _____

    _____

    8. For how long has this disease been known? _____

    _____

    9. Is it found in our state? _____

   10. Have you ever seen an animal with this disease? _____

       If so, describe it. _____

    _____

REFERENCES

Name of book/article	Author	Publisher of book or name of magazine	Pages	Copyright or date of magazine

GUIDE TO FOREIGN FOODS   10–3

     To complete this assignment, you will use books of recipes from foreign countries. Foreign cuisine is featured also in some magazines.

     To find recipes and articles about international cuisine, use such subject headings as COOKERY, FRENCH.

     Your search for information about a specific country's customs can start with subject headings such as FRANCE—SOCIAL LIFE AND CUSTOMS.

     Do not overlook audiovisual programs on your topic, vertical files, and magazine indexes.

     To find useful maps, use a subject heading such as FRANCE—MAPS.

Atlases are located _____

If you are a browser, this information will be helpful:

Recipe books are cataloged _____

Geography, description, and travel materials are cataloged _____

_____

Other references that should be helpful are:

_____

_____

_____

Name _____ Class _____

Date _____

ASSIGNMENT FOR FOREIGN FOODS

Your report is to be typed, prepared on a word processor, or written in either blue or black ink. Use only one side of each sheet of paper. Written information must be presented in paragraph form.

Due date: _____

1. MAP: Trace a map of the country chosen onto letter-size paper. Indicate a minimum of three cities. Indicate regions or provinces within the country. Indicate topography by conventional color coding.

2. MAJOR AGRICULTURAL PRODUCTS: List food and nonfood products. Indicate the value of exports.

3. DISTINCT CUISINE: Describe the distinct cuisine of the major regions, or the entire country if regional cuisine is not applicable.

4. DINNER MENU: Compose a dinner menu that would be representative of this country.

5. HOLIDAY FOODS AND CUSTOMS: Tell about one or two national holidays and the food or food customs associated with them.

6. DAILY MEAL PATTERNS: Describe when and how meals are usually served. Describe the rules of dining etiquette.

7. COMMON FOODS AND RECIPES: Describe a *minimum* of ten ingredients commonly used.

8. RECIPE PREPARED AT HOME: Prepare a typical recipe from this country within the limits of your family budget and food preferences and within the limits of your skill. Bring a small sample of this recipe to class on a paper plate and labeled with your name and the name of the recipe.

9. COPY OF RECIPE: Submit with your report a copy of the recipe you prepared.

10. BIBLIOGRAPHY: Your information must be drawn from a *minimum* of three sources. List these references in proper form on a separate sheet at the end of your report.

GUIDE FOR VISITING ANOTHER LIBRARY   10–5

Classification ''systems'' in libraries are, quite simply, schemes for organizing materials so that those of similar subject matter will be located near one another.

The designations for location indicate where the materials are shelved or housed. The two most frequently used schemes for classifying materials are the Dewey Decimal System and the Library of Congress system.

For example, for the book *Discovering Music* by Roy Hemming, here is how each classification system would designate the book:

	DEWEY DECIMAL	*LIBRARY OF CONGRESS*
Class #	798.9	ML111
		.5
Author	HEM	.H44

The files that tell you what materials are in the library, or in the library system in the case of a network, may be in many different forms. The most common is the card catalog where the information is printed on $3'' \times 5''$ cards that are then interfiled for the public to use. Some files are now prepared on microforms, laser discs, and other computerized data files. Computerized files can be shared via electronic networks with other libraries.

Some large libraries keep their materials in ''closed stacks'' and retrieve them at your request. Generally, however, once you have found the classification symbols for the materials, you can locate them for yourself.

Many libraries, particularly special research libraries, require that you use their resources *in* the library. Most every library has some material that may not be borrowed.

Microform back files of magazines save space and provide quick access to information. You must, of course, use microform readers to view this material.

''Subject headings'' or ''descriptors'' provide access to information whether the method is by card catalog, a computer, or an index to particular sources.

With the rapid increase in sources of information, it is easy to miss some which might better serve your needs. Look carefully for signs that direct you to materials in the library. Seek out the library media specialist for assistance. Members of the staff are still your best source of information!

10–6 ASSIGNMENT FOR VISITING ANOTHER LIBRARY

You are to visit a library media center other than one of the public school libraries in our district. This may be a school library in another district, a public library, a college library, or a special research library.

The subject of your search for information is: _____

_____

The name of the library visited: _____

_____

Date of the visit: _____

Start your research by finding the answers to the following questions:

1. The materials in this library are organized according to:

    _____ Dewey Decimal System of classification

    _____ Library of Congress classification system

    _____ Other: _____

2. Books are housed:

    _____ In open stacks (shelving)

    _____ In closed stacks

    _____ Other: _____

3. The subject heading authority for classifying materials is:

    _____ Sears

    _____ Library of Congress

    _____ Other: _____

4. Materials in the collection are located by using:

    _____ The card catalog

    _____ A book catalog

    _____ A catalog on microfiche

Name _____   Class _____

Date _____

_____ Computer database

_____ Other: _____

5. The periodical indexes available are:

   _____ *Readers' Guide to Periodical Literature*

   _____ *Social Science Index*

   _____ *Applied Science and Technology Index*

   _____ *Business Periodicals Index*

   _____ *Art Index*

   _____ Other: _____

6. Back files of periodicals are:

   _____ Bound

   _____ Microform

   _____ Other: _____

7. The data files available on computer are:

   _____

   _____

   _____

8. These materials do not circulate from this library:

   _____

   _____

   _____

9. The library is a member of a network:

   _____ Yes; name it _____

   _____ No

10–6 cont'd.

10. Interlibrary loan of materials is available:

_____ Yes

_____ No

11. This library is open at the following times:

_____

_____

12. Two magazine articles about my subject are:

_____

_____

_____

_____

13. Two reference books with information about my subject are:

_____

_____

_____

_____

JUNE BULLETIN BOARDS

Flag Day
Father's Day
Children's Day
World Environment Day
Magna Charta Day
Library Bill of Rights Day
United Nations Charter Day

There *Is* Life After High School

June is a time of goodbyes. It seems a propitious time to remind those students who are leaving the school that they will not be forgotten. A caption for your bulletin board is: THERE *IS* LIFE AFTER HIGH SCHOOL.

To prepare this display, you will need to obtain information from your guidance office about the graduates of the preceding year (or years, if your school is small). Where are former students now located? What are they doing?

For this bulletin board, you will need:

- Large sheets of white or gray and black construction paper
- Contrasting small sheets for the letters in the title
- Colored pins

Prepare a large map of the United States, with states and major cities designated. This may be done using the method of enlargement with an overhead projector or an opaque projector. You may have to prepare drawings of foreign countries, also. Center your large map on the bulletin board, and surround it with the foreign countries. Your maps should be on pale construction paper, mounted against a deep-colored background. The letters for the caption can be in contrasting light colors.

Identify the states and countries with a felt-tip marker. Use colored pins to indicate the location of students. Type the students' names and occupations, and cut these into strips. Attach the strips to the locations with the pins.

INSERVICE AND PUBLIC RELATIONS: HOSTING A TEA AND PROMOTING SUMMER LOAN

A pleasant way to finish the school year, and spread cheer to students and staff, is to host an after-school tea in the media center. You might choose from one of several groups to invite, or plan to host more than one such occasion.

Your teas might honor the following people:

- The departing class
- Those students *and* their parents
- The media center volunteers (adults)

- The media center student workers or volunteers
- Parent-teacher officers and staff
- Schoolwide volunteers
- Support staff and teaching staff
- The incoming fall class and their parents

Your principal should be consulted about your plans; if you have no petty cash for the supplies required for a tea, he or she may help you out. The school administrators should be invited to join you no matter what group you invite.

Your art department may be happy to prepare invitations in class.

Arrange for music in the media center at the time of the tea. Take slide photographs of the affair, with the idea that they can be used in your fall orientation programs. If you have video equipment, ask a student or staff member to record the activity on tape.

If your budget will allow, a carnation for each guest of honor will make a wonderful impression.

Throughout this final month of the year it is a good idea to display your most attractive books and advertise summer loan to students and staff. Staff, in particular, will appreciate this opportunity to take home those titles they want to read for pleasure, or curriculum-related materials (including software) they have not found time to study during the year.

Since you must necessarily be working to retrieve overdue materials before students leave, it is important to project as well the positive image of summer borrowing.

Appendix:
Forms to Use in Your
Library Media Center

- Preparing for Opening Day
- Forms to Be Duplicated
- Equipment Request
- Staff Schedule
- Equipment Dispatch Log
- Daily Equipment Sign-Up Sheet
- Daily Newspaper Log
- Video Playback Request
- Periodical Records
- Equipment Inventory Record
- Sample Brochure
- Commercially Prepared Card Catalog Cards
- In-house Computer-Generated Card Catalog Cards
- Cataloging Videotapes
- Cataloging Computer Input
- Invitation to Inservice Presentation on Equipment Use
- Tips for Using Audiovisual Equipment
- Periodical Routing Memo
- Routing Slips
- Periodical Routing Slips
- Periodical Requests
- Film/Video Circulation Record
- Overdue Notice
- Letter to Parents Re: Overdue Materials
- Letter to Parents Re: Overdue Materials
- Notices to Faculty Re: Overdue Materials

- Memos to Faculty Re: Overdue Materials
- Budget Summary Sheet
- Budget Allotment Worksheet
- The Search Strategy
- Vertical File Request Slips
- Records Inventory
- Records Retention/Disposal Schedule
- SIRS Requests
- Evaluation of Previewed Material
- Memo to Faculty Re: Previewed Material
- Letter to Accompany Returned Previewed Materials
- Interlibrary Loan Periodical and Book Requests
- Interlibrary Loan Log
- Database Searching
- Requesting Free Materials
- Requesting Materials from *Vertical File Index*
- Request for Rental Films/Videos
- Request for Videotaping
- Policies and Procedures for Selecting Textbooks, Library Resources, and Other Instructional Materials
- Request for Reconsideration of Instructional Materials
- Notice of Arrival of Recommended Materials
- Memo Re: Erasure of Videotaped Program
- Inventory Record
- Repair Slips
- Sample Storyboard

Preparing for Opening Day

Tasks	Completed	Comments
1. Inspect facility		
2. Select forms to be duplicated		
3. Supply work stations		

4. Post:
   Rules of conduct
   Map of school
   Daily schedule
   Calendar
   Fire drill instructions
   Menu		

5. Prepare and distribute media staff schedule		
6. Distribute hardware to faculty		
7. Create bulletin board		

8. Post at main desk:
   Media staff schedule
   Newspaper log
   Weekly schedule
   Calendar
   Homeroom teacher list		

9. Other		

Forms to Be Duplicated

Forms to Be Duplicated	Date Sent	Date Received
Periodical requests		
Equipment requests		
Newspaper log		
Media staff schedule		
Hardware inventory record		
SIRS charge slips		
Vertical file charge slips		
Routing slips		
Film sign-out sheets		
Periodical inventory cards		
Equipment delivery record		
Interlibrary loan request		
Media center use schedule		
Search requests		
Video playback requests		
Other		

Equipment Request

EQUIPMENT REQUEST

User's Name _____

Today's Date _____

Date(s) Needed _____ Room _____

Periods Needed _____

Please check equipment requested:

16MM Projector _____ Slide Projector _____

Extension Cord _____ Cart _____

Portable Screen _____ Overhead Projector _____

Filmstrip Projector _____ Filmstrip Viewer _____

Record Player _____ Tape recorder _____

Cassette Player _____ Cassette Recorder _____

TV Monitor _____ Opaque Projector _____

VCR _____ Other _____
      1/2"   3/4"

Please request equipment 24 hours in advance of date needed.

Media Center Staff Schedule

TIME	(staff ------)				

Date Issued _____

Equipment Dispatch Log

Date _____

Deliver Equipment	Room	Pick-up Equipment	Room

Daily Equipment Sign-up Sheet

Date _____

Teacher	Room No.	Equipment and Number	Periods Needed	Delivered	Returned

Daily Newspaper Log

Title

Date (√)

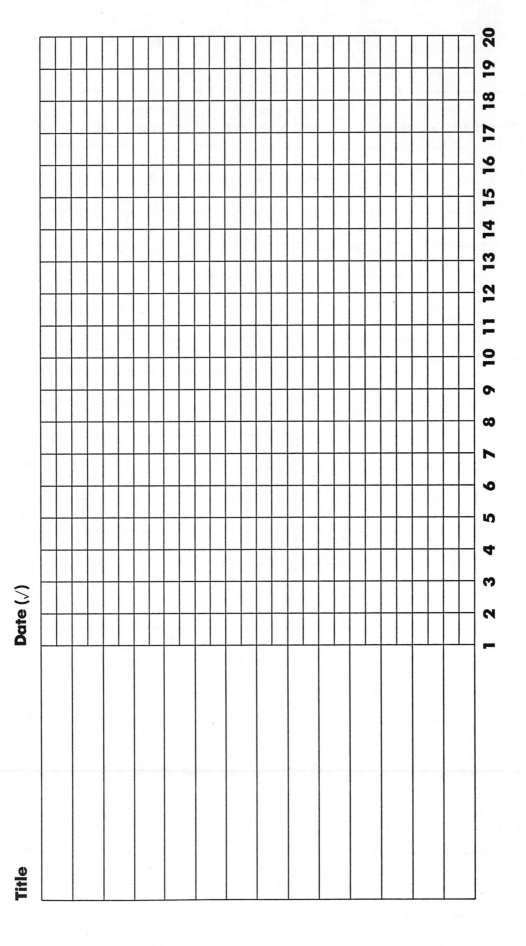

1 2 3 4 5 6 7 8 9 10 11 12 13 14 15 16 17 18 19 20

Video Playback Request

Teacher _____

Title of Tape _____ Number _____

Date _____

Starting Time _____ Viewed in Room _____

Stopping Time _____

Date _____

Starting Time _____ Viewed in Room _____

Stopping Time _____

Date _____

Starting Time _____ Viewed in Room _____

Stopping Time _____

Date _____

Starting Time _____ Viewed in Room _____

Stopping Time _____

If the tape is not housed in our collection, we need to know:

    1. How will it be delivered to us? _____

    2. Is it 3/4" or 1/2" ? (Circle one)

Periodical Records

I.

(Title)					(Date: 1st issue)						
(Term of subscription)					(Frequency)						
(Subscription price)					(Price per issue)						
Year	Jan	Feb	Mar	Apr	May	Jun	Jul	Aug	Sep	Oct	Nov	Dec

II.

(Title)					(Date: 1st issue)						
(Term of subscription)					(Frequency)						
(Subscription price)					(Price per issue)						
Year	Jan	Feb	Mar	Apr	May	Jun	Jul	Aug	Sep	Oct	Nov	Dec
1												
2												
3												
4												
5												
Year												
1												
2												
3												
4												
5												

Equipment Inventory Record

Item _____

Location _____
(School)

Manufacturer _____ Model _____

Serial Number _____ Cost _____

Vendor _____

Date purchased _____

Check (√) condition at inventory:

Year	New	Good	Fair	Poor	Repaired	Retired

1   2   3   4   5   6   7   8

SAMPLE BROCHURES

BETHLEHEM CENTRAL HIGH SCHOOL

MEDIA CENTER

STAFF

RESOURCES

SERVICES

FACILITIES

STAFF

Jane
Streiff
Library/Media
Specialist

Ellen
Dagneau
Library/Media
Specialist

Nicolas
Nealon
Media Technician

Rosemary
Brown
Secretary

Kathy
Blanchard
Media Aide

BETHLEHEM
CENTRAL
TELE-
VISION
CABLE CHANNEL EIGHT
WEEKNIGHTS
7:00 pm TO 8:00 pm

THIS PUBLICATION WAS PRODUCED IN THE
BCHS VIDEO LAB

FACILITIES

The Media Center
is comprised of:

A MAIN AREA
which is furnished
with tables, carrels
and lounge chairs.
It also contains:
* Open Stacks of
  Books
* Copier
* Vertical Files
* Microfilm and
  Microfiche Read-
  ers and Files of
  Microforms
* Circulation Desk
  and Security
  System

A REFERENCE
ROOM

An AUDIO-VISUAL
OFFICE

A MEDIA STAFF
WORKROOM
with A/V Software,
Periodical Back Files,
and Staff Work Sta-
tions.

A MEZZANINE
with A/V Carrels,
TV Reception and a
Classroom Area fur-
nished with Desks and
Chairs for Library Re-
search and Instruction

HOURS
7:30 - 3:30

SAMPLE BROCHURES

AUDIO-VISUAL SERVICES

❋ Ordering and Scheduling Films and Videotapes
 :: 16MM FILM LIBRARY
 :: FREE-LOAN FILMS
 :: RENTAL FILMS

❋ Video Playback
 • IN-HOUSE CLOSED-CIRCUIT TV

❋ A/V Equipment Delivery

❋ Technical Production Assistance

❋ Minor Equipment Repair

❋ In-service Training in Equipment Usage

❋ Videotaping of Classes and Activities

❋ Previewing of Materials

❋ Interfacing Non-print Materials into Curriculum

CALL
EXT
281

RESOURCES
Print and Non-print

❋ Books, A/V Software, Computer Software
 ❋ CLASSIFIED BY DEWEY DECIMAL
 ❋ ACCESSED BY TITLE, AUTHOR, SUBJECT HEADING

❋ Videotapes
 ❋ ACCESSED BY TITLE AND SUBJECT
 ❋ CATALOG IN AUDIO-VISUAL OFFICE

❋ Magazines
 ❋❋ 130-150 TITLES
 ❋❋ FIVE-YEAR FILES IN PRINT
 ❋❋ SELECTED BACK FILES ON MICROFILM

❋ Newspapers
 ❋ 5-7 TITLES
 ❋ BACK ISSUES SAVED ONE MONTH

❋ Microfiche
 ❋❋ NEWSBANK CURRENT EVENTS
 ❋❋ GREAT WRITERS
 ❋❋ SCIENTIFIC ADVENTURES

❋ Vertical Files (pamphlets, etc.)
 • SUBJECT ACCESS THROUGH CARD CATALOG

❋ Paperbacks of Popular Titles

❋ Audio-Visual Equipment

❋ Professional Books and Journals

LIBRARY/MEDIA SERVICES

❋ Orientation to the Media Center

❋ Reference Service

❋ Research Skills Instruction

❋ Ordering Materials for Preview

❋ Scheduling Mezzanine Use

❋ Compiling Bibliographies

❋ Scheduling Use of the Exhibit Area

❋ Magazine Routing

❋ Reserve Collections

❋ Providing Selection Tools

❋ Interlibrary Loans

❋ ERIC Documents

❋ Lesson Plans Enrichment

CALL
EXT
284

Commercially Prepared Cataloging

TITLE CARD ——————

```
158.1    Zilbergeld, Bernie.
Z            Mind power : getting what you want
         through mental training / Bernie
         Zilbergeld, Arnold A. Lazarus. --
         1st ed. -- Boston : Little, Brown,
         c1987.
            ix, 225 p. ; 22 cm.

            Bibliography: p. 224-225.
            ISBN 0-316-98790-5


            1. Success.  2. Mental discipline.
         3. Imagery (Psychology)  I. Lazarus,
         Arnold A.  II. Title.
BF637.S8Z55 1987              158'.1
                                        87-4149
                                      AACR2 MARC

   Library of Congress
00907      07     452900                    7268
```

AUTHOR OR
MAIN ENTRY CARD ——————

```
158.1    Zilbergeld, Bernie.
Z            Mind power : getting what you want
         through mental training / Bernie
         Zilbergeld, Arnold A. Lazarus. --
         1st ed. -- Boston : Little, Brown,
         c1987.
            ix, 225 p. ; 22 cm.

                                $15.45 09/24/87
            Bibliography: p. 224-225.
            ISBN 0-316-98790-5

            1. Success.  2. Mental discipline.
         3. Imagery (Psychology)  I. Lazarus,
         Arnold A.  II. Title.
BF637.S8Z55 1987              158'.1
                                        87-4149
                                      AACR2 MARC

   Library of Congress
00907      07     452900        B           7268
```

SHELF CARD ——————

```
                    Mind power.

158.1    Zilbergeld, Bernie.
Z            Mind power : getting what you want
         through mental training / Bernie
         Zilbergeld, Arnold A. Lazarus. --
         1st ed. -- Boston : Little, Brown,
         c1987.
            ix, 225 p. ; 22 cm.

            Bibliography: p. 224-225.
            ISBN 0-316-98790-5


            1. Success.  2. Mental discipline.
         3. Imagery (Psychology)  I. Lazarus,
         Arnold A.  II. Title.
BF637.S8Z55 1987              158'.1
                                        87-4149
                                      AACR2 MARC

   Library of Congress
00907      07     452900                    7268
```

Commercially Prepared Cataloging (*cont'd.*)

SUBJECT CARD ————

```
                    SUCCESS.

    158.1     Zilbergeld, Bernie.
    Z              Mind power : getting what you want
               through mental training / Bernie
               Zilbergeld, Arnold A. Lazarus. --
               1st ed. -- Boston : Little, Brown,
               c1987.
                    ix, 225 p. ; 22 cm.

                    Bibliography: p. 224-225.
                    ISBN 0-316-98790-5


                    1. Success.  2. Mental discipline.
               3. Imagery (Psychology)  I. Lazarus,
               Arnold A.  II. Title.
    BF637.S8Z55 1987              158'.1
                                           87-4149
                                        AACR2 MARC
         Library of Congress
    00907     07     452900                    7268
```

SUBJECT CARD ————

```
                MENTAL DISCIPLINE.

    158.1     Zilbergeld, Bernie.
    Z              Mind power : getting what you want
               through mental training / Bernie
               Zilbergeld, Arnold A. Lazarus. --
               1st ed. -- Boston : Little, Brown,
               c1987.
                    ix, 225 p. ; 22 cm.

                    Bibliography: p. 224-225.
                    ISBN 0-316-98790-5


                    1. Success.  2. Mental discipline.
               3. Imagery (Psychology)  I. Lazarus,
               Arnold A.  II. Title.
    BF637.S8Z55 1987              158'.1
                                           87-4149
                                        AACR2 MARC
         Library of Congress
    00907     07     452900                    7268
```

SUBJECT CARD ————

```
                IMAGERY (PSYCHOLOGY)

    158.1     Zilbergeld, Bernie.
    Z              Mind power : getting what you want
               through mental training / Bernie
               Zilbergeld, Arnold A. Lazarus. --
               1st ed. -- Boston : Little, Brown,
               c1987.
                    ix, 225 p. ; 22 cm.

                    Bibliography: p. 224-225.
                    ISBN 0-316-98790-5


                    1. Success.  2. Mental discipline.
               3. Imagery (Psychology)  I. Lazarus,
               Arnold A.  II. Title.
    BF637.S8Z55 1987              158'.1
                                           87-4149
                                        AACR2 MARC
         Library of Congress
    00907     07     452900                    7268
```

Source: The Baker & Taylor Co. Reprinted with Permission.

Commercially Prepared Cataloging (*cont'd.*)

ADDED ENTRY CARD

```
             Lazarus, Arnold A.
158.1    Zilbergeld, Bernie.
Z             Mind power : getting what you want
         through mental training / Bernie
         Zilbergeld, Arnold A. Lazarus. --
         1st ed. -- Boston : Little, Brown,
         c1987.
             ix, 225 p. ; 22 cm.

             Bibliography: p. 224-225.
             ISBN 0-316-98790-5


             1. Success.  2. Mental discipline.
         3. Imagery (Psychology)  I. Lazarus,
         Arnold A.  II. Title.
BF637.S8Z55 1987              158'.1
                                        87-4149
                                       AACR2 MARC
Library of Congress
00907    07    452900       THE BAKER & TAYLOR    7268
```

Source: The Baker & Taylor Co. Reprinted with Permission.

NOTE: These are computer-generated cards. Location of the record is noted on the shelf card.

```
SFS
593.71    Hydra life cycle. -- (sound filmstrip) #52-4212.
HYD          -- Carolina Biological Supply Co., 1973.
           1 fs.,col., 52 fr.; 1 cass., 0:15 min.
          audible and inaudible signal, 1 manual.




             1. Hydra.
```

```
SFS
593.71    Hydra life cycle. -- (sound filmstrip) #52-4212.
HYD          -- Carolina Biological Supply Co., 1973.
           1 fs.,col., 52 fr.; 1 cass., 0:15 min.
          audible and inaudible signal, 1 manual.
86-14 | $39.50




DISK12    1. Hydra.
  26
```

```
          HYDRA
SFS
593.71    Hydra life cycle. -- (sound filmstrip) #52-4212.
HYD          -- Carolina Biological Supply Co., 1973.
           1 fs.,col., 52 fr.; 1 cass., 0:15 min.
          audible and inaudible signal, 1 manual.




             1. Hydra.
```

Worksheet for Cataloging Videotapes

TITLE: _____ No. ____
SERIES: _____
SOURCE: _____

FORMAT
____ 1/2" VHS
____ 3/4"
____ 1/2" r/r

____ Time   ____ B/W
____ Cue   ____ Color

SUBJECT: _____

TITLE: _____ No. ____
SERIES: _____
SOURCE: _____

FORMAT
____ 1/2" VHS
____ 3/4"
____ 1/2" r/r

____ Time   ____ B/W
____ Cue   ____ Color

SUBJECT: _____

TITLE: _____ No. ____
SERIES: _____
SOURCE: _____

FORMAT
____ 1/2" VHS
____ 3/4"
____ 1/2" r/r

____ Time   ____ B/W
____ Cue   ____ Color

SUBJECT: _____

TITLE: _____ No. ____
SERIES: _____
SOURCE: _____

FORMAT
____ 1/2" VHS
____ 3/4"
____ 1/2" r/r

____ Time   ____ B/W
____ Cue   ____ Color

SUBJECT: _____

TITLE: _____ No. ____
SERIES: _____
SOURCE: _____

FORMAT
____ 1/2" VHS
____ 3/4"
____ 1/2" r/r

____ Time   ____ B/W
____ Cue   ____ Color

SUBJECT: _____

TITLE: _____ No. ____
SERIES: _____
SOURCE: _____

FORMAT
____ 1/2" VHS
____ 3/4"
____ 1/2" r/r

____ Time   ____ B/W
____ Cue   ____ Color

SUBJECT: _____

Cataloging Computer Input

Print all information

CLASSIFICATION AREA: #1 _____ (Typist: Leave 1st line
#2 _____ blank unless R or OVERSIZE)
#3 _____
#4 _____

AUTHOR (Inverted order) _____
(Example: Galsworthy, John, 1867-1933)

TITLE _____
(150 characters. A semicolon should precede a subtitle)

RESPONSIBILITY _____
(80 characters. Example: edited by William Harris)

EDITION _____
(Example: 1st American edition)

MATERIAL _____
(Serial publications or cartographic materials)

PUBLICATION _____
(Example: New York: Random House, 1982)

PHYSICAL DESCRIPTION _____
(Example: 378p. : ill. ; 27cm.)

SERIES _____
(Enter only if series card is desired; otherwise put in NOTE)

NOTE _____
(Example: Bibliography : p. 165-168)

ANALYTICS _____
(Titles of works in a collection)

ISBN _____   LC # _____

SUBJECTS   1 _____   3 _____

2 _____   4 _____

(Typist: Do not type in numbers or Roman numerals)

ADDED ENTRIES   I _____   III _____

II _____   IV _____

ACCESSION NUMBER _____
(12 characters)

VENDOR _____
(48 characters; include cost)

Invitation to Inservice Presentation on Equipment Use

Media Center   Date _____
Memo To Faculty

Have you ever felt like kicking a machine?
    The media center staff has a prescription for that problem.

    We are offering a series of _____ inservice workshops designed to make YOU more proficient, and less frustrated, when you use audiovisual equipment.

    Session _____ will include the types of equipment checked off below:

_____ 16mm projector

_____ sound filmstrip projector

_____ slide projector

_____ audiocassette recorder

_____ overhead projector

_____ opaque projector

_____ phonograph

_____ videocassette recorder

_____ filmstrip projector

_____ television camera

_____ Other

_____

See you at _____ o'clock

Date _____

Place _____

Tips for Using Audiovisual Equipment

1. Request equipment in advance.

   (Forms are available _____)

2. Place it properly to ensure a smooth presentation.

3. See that it works.

4. Adjust controls for projection and sound.

5. Keep electrical cords out of traffic.

6. Prepare the room: Seating, screen, lighting.

7. Organize your audiovisual material.

8. If there is a problem with operation:

   a. check power

   b. check instructions

   c. do not panic

   d. do not force any parts

   e. call _____ for assistance

9. Rewind films, video, filmstrips, and audio components.

10. Remove materials from machine after use.

11. Retract and secure cords; replace covers.

12. Return audiovisual programs to media center
    (Do not forget manuals, scripts, guides, etc.)

PERIODICAL ROUTING MEMO

Date _____

The Media Center is offering a service whereby you can have selected magazines routed to you or you may see the tables of contents to determine whether you wish to request a particular issue.

If you wish to take advantage of this service, look over the attached list of magazines to which we subscribe, fill out the form below, and return it to the media center. A few magazines are kept for reading in the media center when they first arrive. In this case, you will receive the magazine when the new issue has arrived to replace it.

Remember when you receive a magazine that others may be on the routing service also. Do honor the due dates.

- -

Your name _____

Date _____

I want the following magazines routed to me as they are available:

_____

_____

_____

_____

_____

I would like to see the tables of contents in the following magazines:

_____

_____

_____

_____

_____

Periodical Request Slips

PERIODICAL REQUEST

_____
Title of Magazine

_____
Issue

_____
Borrower's Name

Homeroom # _____

Date Due:

PERIODICAL REQUEST

_____
Title of Magazine

_____
Issue

_____
Borrower's Name

Homeroom # _____

Date Due:

PERIODICAL REQUEST

_____
Title of Magazine

_____
Issue

_____
Borrower's Name

Homeroom # _____

Date Due:

PERIODICAL REQUEST

_____
Title of Magazine

_____
Issue

_____
Borrower's Name

Homeroom # _____

Date Due:

Routing Slips

ROUTING SLIP

Route To: _____ Due: _____

_____ _____

_____ _____

_____ _____

_____ _____

_____ _____

Number of reserves on this material: ___

LOAN PERIOD

____ Overnight

____ Three days

____ One week

MEDIA CENTER

ROUTING SLIP

Route To: _____ Due: _____

_____ _____

_____ _____

_____ _____

_____ _____

_____ _____

Number of reserves on this material: ___

LOAN PERIOD

____ Overnight

____ Three days

____ One week

MEDIA CENTER

ROUTING SLIP

Route To: _____ Due: _____

_____ _____

_____ _____

_____ _____

_____ _____

_____ _____

Number of reserves on this material: ___

LOAN PERIOD

____ Overnight

____ Three days

____ One week

MEDIA CENTER

ROUTING SLIP

Route To: _____ Due: _____

_____ _____

_____ _____

_____ _____

_____ _____

_____ _____

Number of reserves on this material: ___

LOAN PERIOD

____ Overnight

____ Three days

____ One week

MEDIA CENTER

Periodical Routing Slips

PERIODICAL ROUTING SLIP Today's date _____ Your name _____ Homeroom _____ _____ MAGAZINE (*Time, Newsweek,* etc.) Date of magazine: _____ month day year pages _____ Vol. # _____ **LIBRARIAN'S COPY**	**PERIODICAL ROUTING SLIP** Today's date _____ Your name _____ Homeroom _____ _____ MAGAZINE (*Time, Newsweek,* etc.) Date of magazine: _____ month day year pages _____ Vol. # _____ **STUDENT'S COPY**
PERIODICAL ROUTING SLIP Today's date _____ Your name _____ Homeroom _____ _____ MAGAZINE (*Time, Newsweek,* etc.) Date of magazine: _____ month day year pages _____ Vol. # _____ **LIBRARIAN'S COPY**	**PERIODICAL ROUTING SLIP** Today's date _____ Your name _____ Homeroom _____ _____ MAGAZINE (*Time, Newsweek,* etc.) Date of magazine: _____ month day year pages _____ Vol. # _____ **STUDENT'S COPY**
PERIODICAL ROUTING SLIP Today's date _____ Your name _____ Homeroom _____ _____ MAGAZINE (*Time, Newsweek,* etc.) Date of magazine: _____ month day year pages _____ Vol. # _____ **LIBRARIAN'S COPY**	**PERIODICAL ROUTING SLIP** Today's date _____ Your name _____ Homeroom _____ _____ MAGAZINE (*Time, Newsweek,* etc.) Date of magazine: _____ month day year pages _____ Vol. # _____ **STUDENT'S COPY**

Film/Video Circulation Record

Film/Video Title	Date	Teacher Sign-out	Teacher Sign-in

Overdue Notice

OVERDUE NOTICE

To:

Homeroom:

From:

Date:

The following material has been requested by a student/faculty member:

_____ This is due on _____ and cannot be renewed.
Please return it on or before the date due.

_____ This is overdue and should be returned immediately.
Thank you for your cooperation.

OVERDUE NOTICE

To:

Homeroom:

From:

Date:

The following material has been requested by a student/faculty member:

_____ This is due on _____ and cannot be renewed.
Please return it on or before the date due.

_____ This is overdue and should be returned immediately.
Thank you for your cooperation.

Letter to Parents Re: Overdue Materials

Dear _____:

_____ has library materials out that are long overdue. We have sent the student a notice about this, but as yet have not had a response.

We are now asking you to help us retrieve the materials listed below. If they are not returned, we will consider them lost, and it will be necessary for us to charge the amount indicated.

I sincerely hope that you can assist us in this matter.

Sincerely yours,

_____

Media Specialist

_____

_____

_____

_____

_____

_____

_____

_____

_____

Letter to Parents Re: Overdue Materials

Dear _____:

    We are writing to solicit your help in retrieving media center material that _____ has not returned.

    The media center contains materials relating to the school curriculum. Many of the titles are used for book reports and projects. Therefore, a student keeping books longer than several days past the due date may be preventing other students from completing their assignments.

    We contact students through their homeroom when materials they have borrowed are overdue. We also remind them in the morning bulletin to return materials.

    Please assist us in making materials available to all our students by encouraging the return of the following materials. If the materials are lost, payment is expected.

_____	$ _____
_____	$ _____
_____	$ _____
_____	$ _____
TOTAL	$ _____

Thank you for your cooperation.

Sincerely,

_____
Media Specialist

Notices to Faculty Regarding Overdue Materials

TO FACULTY/STAFF:

FROM: MEDIA CENTER

DATE:

RE: Library materials charged to you.

According to our records you have the following materials which are overdue. Please return those you are no longer using.

_____

_____

_____

_____

TO FACULTY/STAFF:

FROM: MEDIA CENTER

DATE:

RE: Library materials charged to you.

According to our records you have the following materials which are overdue. Please return those you are no longer using.

_____

_____

_____

_____

Memos to Faculty Re: Overdue Materials

TO:

FROM:

DATE:

RE: Students with overdue library materials as posted in homerooms.

Please have the following students report to me during homeroom on

_____.

Thank you.

_____

_____

_____

_____

TO:

FROM:

DATE:

RE: Students with overdue library materials as posted in homerooms.

Please have the following students report to me during homeroom on

_____.

Thank you.

_____

_____

_____

_____

Budget Summary Sheet

Budget Year _____ To _____

Code	Description	Allotment
Additional Funds		

Comments:

Budget Allotment Worksheet

Year _____

Budget Code _____

Allotment _____

PO No.	Date	Vendor	Amount	Balance	Invoice Amount	New Balance

HOW TO RESEARCH & FIND INFORMATION IN THE LIBRARY

1. The key to finding information in the Library is to formulate a *Search Strategy.* A Search Strategy is a method of checking the most important areas in the Library that contain information for your needs.

2. The (5) important information areas are:
(Books, Periodicals, Newspapers, Vertical Files & Supplemental Sources).

3. The Librarian is there to help *you* with your Search Strategy.

THE SEARCH STRATEGY

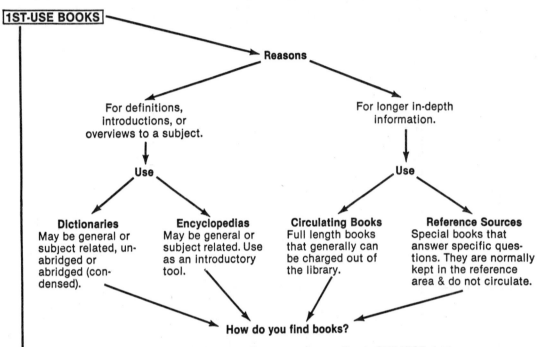

1ST-USE BOOKS

Reasons

For definitions, introductions, or overviews to a subject.

For longer in-depth information.

Use

Use

Dictionaries
May be general or subject related, un-abridged or abridged (condensed).

Encyclopedias
May be general or subject related. Use as an introductory tool.

Circulating Books
Full length books that generally can be charged out of the library.

Reference Sources
Special books that answer specific questions. They are normally kept in the reference area & do not circulate.

How do you find books?

1. Use the catalog. It is usually arranged according to SUBJECT, Author, & Title. Remember SAT. (SUBJECT, Author, & Title)
2. The SUBJECT approach will give you an inventory or listing (bibliography) of the books that your library contains on that SUBJECT.
3. Be sure that you understand the catalog. If not, see the librarian.
4. If you are not finding information, you are probably using the catalog incorrectly. See the librarian for assistance.

2ND-USE PERIODICAL ARTICLES

Reasons

1. This type of information is brief and up-to-date.
2. They up-date information found in books.
3. They may provide information not found in books.

(over)

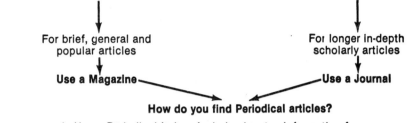

For brief, general and popular articles

Use a Magazine

For longer in-depth scholarly articles

Use a Journal

How do you find Periodical articles?

1. Use a Periodical Index. An index locates information for you.
2. These indexes are usually arranged alphabetically by subject and can be general or subject related in coverage.
3. Ask the librarian where these indexes are shelved and how they work.

3RD-USE NEWSPAPER ARTICLES

Reasons

1. Contain current as well as retrospective (historical) information.
2. Answer the questions of who, why, what, when, where, and how.

How do you find Newspaper articles?

1. Use a Newspaper Index. An index locates information for you.
2. These indexes are usually arranged alphabetically by subject and chronologically according to the calendar year within that subject.
3. Ask the librarian where the Newspaper indexes are shelved and how they work.

4TH-USE VERTICAL FILE INFORMATION (Pamphlets)

Reasons

1. Information contained in these files is usually "non-shelvable."
2. Formats include pamphlets, booklets, news clippings, etc.

How do you find Vertical File information?

1. Look for catalog of SUBJECT headings near the Vertical file cabinets.
2. If you can't locate the catalog or cabinets containing these files, ask the librarian for assistance.

5TH-USE SUPPLEMENTAL SOURCES

Reasons

1. These areas may contain information not previously found.
2. These sources may supplement or complete your information needs.
3. *Not* all libraries have these additional areas. Ask your librarian.

Audio-Visual
May contain information in the form of slides, films, video & audio tapes, film-strips, etc.

Interlibrary Loan
If your library belongs to a system of librar-ies, it may be possible to interloan books, periodicals, etc., from these other libraries.

Government Documents
Many local, state, & federal government agencies publish impor-tant information in the form of books, reports, periodicals, pamphlets, etc.

Computer Data Base Access
Your library may have a com-puter terminal that is linked to various data bases con-taining information. See your librarian for details.

Published by Business Answers, 83 Bayberry Dr., Huntington, NY, 11743
(Permission is granted to reproduce this document)

Vertical File Request Slip

VERTICAL FILE REQUEST SLIP Folder _____ _____ Number of items _____ Borrower's name: _____ Homeroom number: _____ Date due: _____ MEDIA CENTER	VERTICAL FILE REQUEST SLIP Folder _____ _____ Number of items _____ Borrower's name: _____ Homeroom number: _____ Date due: _____ MEDIA CENTER
VERTICAL FILE REQUEST SLIP Folder _____ _____ Number of items _____ Borrower's name: _____ Homeroom number: _____ Date due: _____ MEDIA CENTER	VERTICAL FILE REQUEST SLIP Folder _____ _____ Number of items _____ Borrower's name: _____ Homeroom number: _____ Date due: _____ MEDIA CENTER

Records Inventory

Document name:	Location:
Inventory number assigned:	Volume (inclusive dates):
Number of parts:	Numbers printed on series:
Purpose:	Blank forms available from:
	Filing supplies used:
How used:	Filing arrangement:
	Filed by:
Format (paper): Letter-size _____ Legal-size _____ Computer _____ One-sided _____ Double-sided _____	Referenced: Daily _____ Weekly _____ Yearly _____ Other: _____
Machine-readable format: Other:	Location of duplicates:
Recommendation for retention:	Inventoried by:
	Inventory date:

Records Retention/Disposal Schedule

Records series title:				
Numbers assigned:		Description:		
Office:		Disposal method:		
Issued by:		Date:		
Document	**Number**	**Removal**	**Disposal**	**Initials**

SIRS Request Slip

SIRS REQUEST

Title _____
    Name of volume

Volume number _____

Article # _____ __, _____

_____, _____, _____

Please submit separate request slips for different titles.

Name _____

Home room _____

Date Due _____

SIRS REQUEST

Title _____
    Name of volume

Volume number _____

Article # _____, _____

_____, _____, _____

Please submit separate request slips for different titles.

Name _____

Home room _____

Date Due _____

SIRS REQUEST

Title _____
    Name of volume

Volume number _____

Article # _____, _____

_____, _____, _____

Please submit separate request slips for different titles.

Name _____

Home room _____

Date Due _____

SIRS REQUEST

Title _____
    Name of volume

Volume number _____

Article # _____, _____

_____, _____, _____

Please submit separate request slips for different titles.

Name _____

Home room _____

Date Due _____

Evaluation of Previewed Material

TITLE _____

FORMAT _____

_____

PUBLISHER _____ COST _____

PREVIEWED BY _____

EVALUATION:	Excellent	Fair	Poor
Potential for use	_____	_____	_____
Compatibility with equipment	_____	_____	_____
Technical quality	_____	_____	_____
Timeliness	_____	_____	_____
Authority	_____	_____	_____
Relationship to curriculum	_____	_____	_____

This material meets my needs: _____ Yes _____ No

I would prefer this material in a different format: _____ Yes _____ No

I recommend this material for purchase: _____ Yes _____ No

Comments:

RETURN MATERIAL AND EVALUATION TO THE MEDIA CENTER BY: _____

Signed: _____

- -

(Tear here and leave bottom portion with media specialist)

TITLE _____

DATE ACQUIRED _____ DATE TO BE SHIPPED _____

PURCHASED _____ RETURNED TO VENDOR _____

Memo to Faculty Re: Previewed Material

MEMO TO:

DATE:

RE: Preview materials signed out to you.

The preview material entitled _____

was signed out to you on _____.

This is a reminder to you that the material and your evaluation are due back in the media

center on _____.

Thank you,

_____

Media Center staff

Letter to Accompany Returned Previewed Materials

Date:

Re: Preview order

Vendor:

Thank you for allowing us to preview the enclosed material.
The evaluations from our staff indicated that it is not
appropriate for our curriculum at this time.

Sincerely yours,

Media Center

Interlibrary Loan Periodical Request

Interlibrary Loan Periodical Request

Name _____ Homeroom number _____

Title of periodical _____

Issue _____ Page(s) _____

Author of article _____

Title of the article _____

The material requested above is:

_____ being held at the circulation desk until _____

_____ unavailable

Ask the person at the circulation desk for the 3″ × 5″ card containing a statement about copyright restrictions. This must be signed for us to forward your request.

Interlibrary Loan Book Request

Name _____ Homeroom number _____

Title of book _____

Author _____

Publisher _____ Copyright date _____

If you will accept a substitute, please give a specific subject:

_____

The material requested above is:

_____ being held at the circulation desk until _____

_____ unavailable

Interlibrary Loan Log

Loaned to	Title	Call No.	Requested for	Home-room No.	Date Rec'd	Date Due

Database Search Request Form

Database Name _____ Date Request _____
(if known)

User Name _____ Date Needed _____

Position _____ Phone _____

Institution _____

Address _____

Subject Request: Please give a complete description of the information needed, including synonyms for technical terms. Define any terms that have special meaning in the context of your request. Indicate any aspects of the subject that are to be *excluded*.

_____

_____

_____

_____

_____

_____

_____

Indicate Preference:

_____ Narrow search with fewer references right on the subject

_____ Broader search with more general references and more complete coverage

Time Period to Be Searched:

_____ Current year only   _____ 3-5 years   _____ other (specify)

Purpose of Search:

_____ Information   _____ Term Paper   _____ Research

_____ Speech   _____ Other_____

For Whom Search Is Being Prepared:

_____ Librarian   _____ Administrator   _____ Faculty

_____ Student (indicate grade level _____)

Requesting Free Materials

Date _____

_____

_____

_____

We would like to receive _____ copy/copies of the free materials entitled:

_____

_____

_____

that were listed in _____.

Thank you for assisting us to enrich the curriculum of our school program.

Sincerely yours,

_____

Media Specialist

Requesting Materials From *Vertical File Index*

Date_____

_____

_____

_____

We would like to receive _____ copy/copies of the free materials entitled:

_____

_____

_____

that are listed in the *Vertical File Index*.

Thank you for assisting us to enrich the curriculum of our school program.

Sincerely yours,

_____

Media Specialist

Request for Rental Films/Videos

Date _____

1. Use a separate form for each film library.

2. List films/videos in chronological order of show dates.

3. Return to the media center by this date: _____

Film library: _____

Your department: _____

Your name: _____

Total cost for this sheet: _____

Catalog Number	Title	Preferred Date	Alternate Date	Cost

Approved By _____

Request for Videotaping

Date of request _____   Requested by _____

Title of program _____

Date needed _____   Time _____ a.m.   Channel _____

_____ p.m.

Return this form to the media center. The media center staff will return it to you when your request has been filled. At that time, please note the information supplied below.

_____ **The following copyright restrictions apply:**

1. The program you requested was taped and is ready for your use.

2. You may use this program in class until this date: _____

3. After that time, you may use it for evaluative purposes until this date: _____

4. The tape will then be erased.

_____ **This material is free of copyright restrictions:**

1. Fair use of this material has been arranged for until this date: _____

2. This tape has been purchased and added to our audiovisual collection.

_____

Policies and Procedures for Selecting Textbooks, Library Resources, and Other Instructional Materials

Legal Responsibility

As the governing body of the school district, the Board of Education shall be legally responsible for the selection and approval of all printed and published materials used in the school district. As the policy-making body, the Board of Education delegates authority to the professional staff for the selection of textbooks, library resources, and other instructional materials.

Objectives of Selection

1. The selection of textbooks, library resources, and other instructional materials shall reflect and help implement the basic functions of a good school program. The materials selected shall:

   a. Provide teachers and pupils with reference and supplementary materials that will support and enrich the curriculum.

   b. Enable and encourage pupils to develop further their full potential as creative and responsible individuals by meeting and stimulating the greatest possible diversity of interests and abilities, whether or not these materials are directly related to the curriculum.

2. To fulfill these two basic functions, endeavor shall be made to provide easy access to a centrally cataloged and comprehensive collection of a variety of materials at appropriate levels of difficulty to:

   a. Evoke a love of reading and learning that will assure a source of continuing self-education and personal enjoyment.
   b. Generate an understanding of our country's freedoms and a desire to preserve those freedoms through the development of informed and responsible citizenship.
   c. Develop reading skills and literary and aesthetic tastes.
   d. Encourage pupils to locate, use, and evaluate as much material as possible on opposing sides of controversial issues so that they may develop, under guidance, the practice of critical examination and thinking.
   e. Fairly represent the many religious, ethnic, and cultural groups and their contribution to our country's heritage.

Criteria for Selection

The criteria for selection of materials shall be:

1. The needs of individual schools and the needs of individual students.

2. Provision of a wide range of materials on all levels of difficulty, with diversity of appeal and the presentation of different points of view.

3. Provision of materials of high artistic quality and with superior format.

4. Provision of materials that possess the qualities of factual accuracy, authoritativeness, balance, and integrity.

Methods of Selection

1. Authoritative selection aids shall be used regularly by the professional staff. These shall be standard guides that are reputable, unbiased, and professionally prepared.

2. Personal examination and evaluation of materials shall be made by the professional staff when possible.

Procedure for Meeting Challenges of Materials

The following procedure shall be used to handle criticisms of selection:

1. Individuals or groups voicing objections shall be offered copies of this statement and copies of "Request for Reconsideration of Instructional Materials."

2. Individuals or groups voicing objections shall be requested to submit their criticisms on the "Request for Reconsideration of Instructional Materials" to the Superintendent. The Board of Education shall be informed; the Professional Rights and Responsibilities Committee of the parent-teacher association shall be informed; and the member(s) of the professional staff involved in the selection of the materials questioned shall be informed.

3. A committee of five shall review complaints and make recommendations to the Board of Education. This committee shall be comprised of the principal of the school involved, the director of curriculum or the Superintendent, and three faculty members who will be appointed by the chairperson of the Professional Rights and Responsibilities Committee.

4. The committee shall judge the challenged material as to its conformity to the above objectives and criteria for selection.

5. The Superintendent shall announce the committee's recommendations regarding the complaint and report them directly to the Board of Education.

Request for Reconsideration of Instructional Materials

Author _____   Type of material _____

Title _____

Publisher (if known) _____

Request initiated by _____   Date _____

Telephone _____   Address _____

City/State _____   ZIP Code _____

Complainant represents: _____ Self

_____ Other group (identify) _____

1. To what do you object? Please be specific. _____
    _____
    _____

2. What do you feel might be the result of using this material? _____
    _____

3. For what age group would you recommend it? _____

4. Is there anything good about it? _____
    _____

5. Did you examine it in full? _____ If not, what parts did you examine?
    _____
    _____

6. Are you aware of professional evaluations of this material? _____
    _____

7. What do you believe is its purpose or theme? _____
    _____

8. What would you like your school to do about this? _____
    _____

9. What would you recommend to replace it? _____
    _____

SUBMIT THIS FORM TO THE SUPERINTENDENT OF SCHOOLS.

Notice of Arrival of Recommended Materials

NOTICE OF ARRIVAL OF RECOMMENDED MATERIALS

To: _____

From: Media Center

Date: _____

RE: Materials recommended for purchase

_____ Book

_____ Audiovisual material

TITLE: _____

This material, which you had recommended, has been received and processed. It will be held for you at the circulation desk until this date _____.

NOTICE OF ARRIVAL OF RECOMMENDED MATERIALS

To: _____

From: Media Center

Date: _____

RE: Materials recommended for purchase

_____ Book

_____ Audiovisual material

TITLE: _____

This material, which you had recommended, has been received and processed. It will be held for you at the circulation desk until this date _____.

Memo Re: Erasure of Videotaped Program

To: _____

From: Media Center

Date: _____

Re: _____
   Video Taped Program

   In compliance with current copyright guidelines, it is now time to erase the program listed above.

   This will be done on _____
                                              Date

   If you feel this program or one of a similar nature should be purchased for the collection, please talk with the media specialist.

Inventory Record

Inventory/Year _____   Media Center

Section	No. of Titles	No. of Volumes	Missing 1 year	Missing 2 years	Missing 3 years	With- drawn
Reference						
SC						
Fiction						
000						
100						
200						
300						
400						
500						
600						
700						
800						
900						
Total Book						
SFS						
AC						
REC						
SSL						
VC						
FS						
SL						
CP						
FL						
F						
Total AV						

1   2   3   4   5   6   7   8

Repair Slip

REPAIR SLIP

Call #

_____

_____   Acc. # _____

_____

Author _____

Title _____

_____

_____ Replace pages
_____ Tape torn pages
_____ Erasures needed
_____ Clean cover
_____ Re-attach cover
_____ Re-mark spine
_____ Replace pocket
_____ Type new card
_____ Send to bindery
_____ Withdraw
_____ Splice film
_____ Replace guide
_____ Other _____

REPAIR SLIP

Call #

_____

_____   Acc. # _____

_____

Author _____

Title _____

_____

_____ Replace pages
_____ Tape torn pages
_____ Erasures needed
_____ Clean cover
_____ Re-attach cover
_____ Re-mark spine
_____ Replace pocket
_____ Type new card
_____ Send to bindery
_____ Withdraw
_____ Splice film
_____ Replace guide
_____ Other _____

REPAIR SLIP

Call #

_____

_____   Acc. # _____

_____

Author _____

Title _____

_____

_____ Replace pages
_____ Tape torn pages
_____ Erasures needed
_____ Clean cover
_____ Re-attach cover
_____ Re-mark spine
_____ Replace pocket
_____ Type new card
_____ Send to bindery
_____ Withdraw
_____ Splice film
_____ Replace guide
_____ Other _____

REPAIR SLIP

Call #

_____

_____   Acc. # _____

_____

Author _____

Title _____

_____

_____ Replace pages
_____ Tape torn pages
_____ Erasures needed
_____ Clean cover
_____ Re-attach cover
_____ Re-mark spine
_____ Replace pocket
_____ Type new card
_____ Send to bindery
_____ Withdraw
_____ Splice film
_____ Replace guide
_____ Other _____

Sample Storyboard

PICTURE

SOUND